Federalism and The Organization of Political Life:
Canada in Comparative Perspective

ISSN 0708-3289
ISBN 0-88911-032-8

JL
15
B3 / 32,849

Queen's Studies on the Future of the Canadian Communities is a monograph
series based on research funded by the Donner Canadian Foundation.

Distributed by P.D. Meany Company Incorporated,
Box 534, Port Credit, Ontario L5G 4M2

Typesetting: Eastern Typesetting Company, Kingston, Ontario

Printed in Canada by: Brown & Martin Limited, Kingston, Ontario

Queen's Studies on the
Future of the
Canadian Communities

2

Federalism and The Organization of Political Life: Canada in Comparative Perspective

Herman Bakvis

Institute of
Intergovernmental
Relations

Queen's University
Kingston, Ontario
Canada

Contents

v

Foreword

This is the second in a series of monographs, published under the general title, Queen's Studies on the Future of the Canadian Communities. The monographs are designed to present research and analysis which at the same time advance our intellectual understanding of the problems of the Canadian federal system and directly focus on the broad political choices which face us.

In this study, Herman Bakvis examines some fundamental questions about the linkages between the nature of communities to which citizens belong, and the ways those communities are reflected in the structure of political institutions. He draws on the experience of societies with patterns of political division analogous to those in Canada, notably Belgium and the Netherlands. He provides a valuable critique of some prominent theories of political integration, notably the model of "consociational democracy". Skillfully weaving different theoretical strands, including theory of conflict, organization theory and others, he draws some persuasive conclusions about the consequences of some of the constitutional proposals recently discussed.

This, like other monographs in this series, has been made possible by a generous grant from the Donner Canadian Foundation.

Herman Bakvis is presently Assistant Professor in public administration and political science at Dalhousie University. His book on the church and politics in the Netherlands is shortly to be published by McGill-Queen's University Press.

Richard Simeon
Director,

Institute of
Intergovernmental Relations,
Queen's University.

Preface

This monograph is concerned with three questions: What kinds of communities make up Canada? How and where are these communities to be given political expression? How can the conflicting interests of these communities be reconciled?

These questions are very much related to the current Canadian dilemma of choosing among alternatives for constitutional change; but they also have wider relevance since the Canadian dilemma is, in many respects, a universal one: other nations, both past and present, federal and non-federal, have faced similar difficulties in searching for appropriate means of giving diverse communities political expression and in mitigating the consequences of conflicting communal interests. This study, therefore, deliberately draws not only on Canadian material but also on the experiences of other countries. My intent is to alter and replace some of the commonplace notions many people have about the nature of political communities — whether based on territory, language, religion, or class — and about the form that political representation and integration should take.

During the past few years several people have helped in shaping the substance of this study. First and foremost, let me thank Ronald L. Watts, Principal of Queen's University, and Richard Simeon, Director of the Institute of Intergovernmental Relations, for inviting me to Queen's for the year 1978-79 to participate in the Future of the Canadian Communities project and, more importantly, for encouraging me to examine critically certain assumptions about federalism. Ronald Watts showed me that it is possible to integrate the old with the new, and that the experiences of the third world can be relevant indeed to understanding Canadian federalism.

Other people at Queen's whom I found both stimulating and good company were Bill Irvine, Phil Goldman, Jim deWilde, Peter Leslie, Jack Grove, Jock Gunn, Paul Lucardie, and Ed Black. Chapter two of this monograph is based in part on a paper presented to the joint CPSA/Israel Workshop on Political Cleavages held in Israel in December 1978. I would like to thank the organizers of that workshop Maurice Pinard and Martin Seliger for having invited me, and the participants for their comments. Also, I would like to thank David Smith of the University of Saskatchewan for asking me to present my ideas on consociationalism to his senior seminar in Canadian government. Some of these ideas evolved to become the basis for chapter three.

Richard Simeon and Bill Irvine improved the manuscript immeasurably by subjecting it to a critical reading, offering suggestions on both style and substance. The manuscript has benefited also from comments by Dave Phillips and Paul Burdett, and from the skillful editing of Mrs. Carol Ann Pentland. Paul Burdett helped compile the bibliography. Finally, I would like to acknowledge the help and encouragement of the staff at the Institute of Intergovernmental Relations, in particular that of Patti Candido, Julia Eastman, and the late Dorothy Holman.

Many people have contributed to this study, both substantively and critically, and I am grateful to them. For any errors of fact or interpretation, however, I will gladly take full responsibility.

Herman Bakvis,
Dalhousie University.

Herman Bakvis is Assistant Professor of Political Science and Public Administration at Dalhousie University. His main interests are comparative federalism, political parties, and electoral behaviour.

ISSN 0708-3289
ISBN 0-88911-032-8

Queen's Studies on the Future of the Canadian Communities is a monograph series based on research funded by the Donner Canadian Foundation.

Distributed by P.D. Meany Company Incorporated,
Box 534, Port Credit, Ontario L5G 4M2

Typesetting: Eastern Typesetting Company, Kingston, Ontario

Printed in Canada by: Brown & Martin Limited, Kingston, Ontario

Queen's Studies on the
Future of the
Canadian Communities

2

Federalism and The Organization of Political Life: Canada in Comparative Perspective

Herman Bakvis

Institute of
Intergovernmental
Relations

Queen's University
Kingston, Ontario
Canada

Contents

Foreword

This is the second in a series of monographs, published under the general title, Queen's Studies on the Future of the Canadian Communities. The monographs are designed to present research and analysis which at the same time advance our intellectual understanding of the problems of the Canadian federal system and directly focus on the broad political choices which face us.

In this study, Herman Bakvis examines some fundamental questions about the linkages between the nature of communities to which citizens belong, and the ways those communities are reflected in the structure of political institutions. He draws on the experience of societies with patterns of political division analogous to those in Canada, notably Belgium and the Netherlands. He provides a valuable critique of some prominent theories of political integration, notably the model of "consociational democracy". Skillfully weaving different theoretical strands, including theory of conflict, organization theory and others, he draws some persuasive conclusions about the consequences of some of the constitutional proposals recently discussed.

This, like other monographs in this series, has been made possible by a generous grant from the Donner Canadian Foundation.

Herman Bakvis is presently Assistant Professor in public administration and political science at Dalhousie University. His book on the church and politics in the Netherlands is shortly to be published by McGill-Queen's University Press.

Richard Simeon
Director,

Institute of
Intergovernmental Relations,
Queen's University.

Preface

This monograph is concerned with three questions: What kinds of communities make up Canada? How and where are these communities to be given political expression? How can the conflicting interests of these communities be reconciled?

These questions are very much related to the current Canadian dilemma of choosing among alternatives for constitutional change; but they also have wider relevance since the Canadian dilemma is, in many respects, a universal one: other nations, both past and present, federal and non-federal, have faced similar difficulties in searching for appropriate means of giving diverse communities political expression and in mitigating the consequences of conflicting communal interests. This study, therefore, deliberately draws not only on Canadian material but also on the experiences of other countries. My intent is to alter and replace some of the commonplace notions many people have about the nature of political communities — whether based on territory, language, religion, or class — and about the form that political representation and integration should take.

During the past few years several people have helped in shaping the substance of this study. First and foremost, let me thank Ronald L. Watts, Principal of Queen's University, and Richard Simeon, Director of the Institute of Intergovernmental Relations, for inviting me to Queen's for the year 1978-79 to participate in the Future of the Canadian Communities project and, more importantly, for encouraging me to examine critically certain assumptions about federalism. Ronald Watts showed me that it is possible to integrate the old with the new, and that the experiences of the third world can be relevant indeed to understanding Canadian federalism.

Other people at Queen's whom I found both stimulating and good company were Bill Irvine, Phil Goldman, Jim deWilde, Peter Leslie, Jack Grove, Jock Gunn, Paul Lucardie, and Ed Black. Chapter two of this monograph is based in part on a paper presented to the joint CPSA/Israel Workshop on Political Cleavages held in Israel in December 1978. I would like to thank the organizers of that workshop Maurice Pinard and Martin Seliger for having invited me, and the participants for their comments. Also, I would like to thank David Smith of the University of Saskatchewan for asking me to present my ideas on consociationalism to his senior seminar in Canadian government. Some of these ideas evolved to become the basis for chapter three.

Richard Simeon and Bill Irvine improved the manuscript immeasurably by subjecting it to a critical reading, offering suggestions on both style and substance. The manuscript has benefited also from comments by Dave Phillips and Paul Burdett, and from the skillful editing of Mrs. Carol Ann Pentland. Paul Burdett helped compile the bibliography. Finally, I would like to acknowledge the help and encouragement of the staff at the Institute of Intergovernmental Relations, in particular that of Patti Candido, Julia Eastman, and the late Dorothy Holman.

Many people have contributed to this study, both substantively and critically, and I am grateful to them. For any errors of fact or interpretation, however, I will gladly take full responsibility.

Herman Bakvis,
Dalhousie University.

Herman Bakvis is Assistant Professor of Political Science and Public Administration at Dalhousie University. His main interests are comparative federalism, political parties, and electoral behaviour.

1 Learning from Comparative Experience

What can we as Canadians learn from the experience of other countries? Currently governmental decision-makers, numerous citizen groups, and others, are examining various options for altering the way we govern ourselves. There have been calls for more decentralization — for greater provincial jurisdiction in fields such as communications and natural resources. Some have called for greater centralization; they would like a stronger federal presence in economic planning, for example. Others would like to see stronger and more representative political parties which would better integrate regional interests at the centre, by-passing the provincial governments. Many political scientists, the New Democratic Party, and the Task Force on Canadian Unity, have all advocated the adoption of a proportional electoral system to help strengthen national political parties.

All these options have been tried and implemented — not in Canada but in other nations. One major reason for looking at Canadian problems in a comparative context is to examine some of the alternatives and how they might operate in Canada. However, we have to be careful: institutions and practices borrowed from abroad may have quite a different effect when placed in the Canadian setting. But here, too, the comparative experience can help us. The second reason for examining other nations is to help us understand the important political forces and processes in Canada. For example, the experience of countries like Belgium, Ireland, Spain, India, and Nigeria, may help pinpoint the causes involved in the rise of ethnic conflict. We can then use this understanding to assess the adequacy of proposals concerning representation of the two major linguistic communities in Canada or to help decide what kind of official recognition should be given to ethnic communities which are neither English nor French.

1

This monograph, therefore, has two aims: (1) to help provide an understanding of the pressures faced by the Canadian federal system, particularly those stemming from the politicization of ethnic, linguistic, and regional cleavages; and (2) to elevate some of the specific proposals for constitutional change, proposals which seek to reconcile the conflicting interests of different regional and linguistic communities in Canada. Cross-national comparisons are used in both instances. But before getting to the substance of conflict and cleavage, and proposals for change, it would be worthwhile to discuss in greater detail the rationale for drawing on the experience of other countries in analyzing Canadian problems, as well as to look at the difficulties which have to be overcome in order to make such comparisons valuable.

A. Why Make Cross-national Comparisons?

Many would argue that the amount of useful information we can acquire through cross-national comparison is limited. Some years ago Kenneth McRae (1973) stated that Canada is unique and therefore difficult to compare with other nations on an overall basis. No country has the same social, economic, and cultural make-up combined with a federal system of government as Canada; no other nation stands in the same relation to a much larger neighbour as Canada. Countries which are linguistically or culturally divided tend to be much smaller than Canada. Countries comparable in terms of geography are either much less developed, for example India, or have a vastly different political system, for example, the Soviet Union. McRae's sentiments are shared by many: most academics studying Canadian politics do not think in comparative terms and neither do the vast majority of Canadians. Presentations made to the hearings held by the Task Force on Canadian Unity, with a few exceptions, rarely made reference to the experience of other countries.[1]

Is there anything at all which can be learned from looking at other federal systems, or even non-federal systems? The rejection or neglect of comparative analysis frequently rests on mistaken assumptions about what the comparative method involves. Much of the work done in the social sciences, and by most people in everyday life, involves making comparisons, if only implicitly. For example the statement that Canada is unique implies comparison; it begs the question, unique with respect to which countries? An answer to this question requires specifying the characteristics of other countries in order to show how Canada differs. To say that Canada is not comparable also imputes to political and social systems characteristics they may not have. As Przeworski and Teune (1970, p. 10) note:

> Social phenomena do not have a property of "being compara-
> ble" or "not comparable". "Comparability" depends upon the
> level of generality of the language that is applied to express
> observations. The response to the classical objection to compar-
> ing "apples and oranges" is simple: they are "fruits".

Thus, the problem of comparison in large part is one of definition. If we define the units of comparison as unique then comparison is impossible. The task becomes easier, however, if we admit that all systems contain within them common characteristics or factors: it is the combination and the number of these characteristics which differ from system to system.

The aim is to understand how the Canadian federal system operates and what the consequences might be if we were to change elements within the system, or the relationships between them, for example by altering the role of the supreme court vis-à-vis the powers held by parliament or introducing proportional representation for the House of Commons. Such a new or revised combination of elements may well exist in some other context and may offer valuable lessons as to the probable consequences of this new arrangement if it were implemented in Canada. For example, some economists have argued for changes in the current Canadian fiscal equalization arrangement. At the moment, the federal government plays an important role in redistributing some of the federal tax revenues to the governments of the "have-not" provinces, thereby ensuring a roughly comparable standard of provincial govern-ment services across the country. It has been suggested that equalization should be left to the provinces; one such scheme would have the richer provinces contribute money to a pool and then the richer provinces, or all ten provinces, would decide amongst themselves how to allocate these monies to the different provincial governments. What might be the consequences? In West Germany, there is a limited form of such an arrangement called "second round" sharing where the Laender (the equivalent of Canadian provinces) decide amongst themselves how to divide up a revenue pool. Experience indicates that invariably the money is shared on an equal per capita basis (Spahn, 1978). Unlike the current Canadian system very little *re*distribution takes place in West Germany.

There would, of course, be several aspects to any equalization scheme run by the provinces, such as reduction of provincial dependency on the federal government; but the West German experience can help in judg-ing the probable consequences of such a new system, at least in certain areas, and ultimately aid in evaluating its overall viability. However, such a comparison between West Germany and Canada involves admit-ting that there are at least certain common characteristics between the two countries, their so-called uniqueness notwithstanding. The latter point is especially important; frequently people will raise objections to cross-national comparisons by invoking the "unique" qualities of systems, qualities which in reality may have very little bearing on the problem at hand. Medical scientists, when they discover that the rate of a particular type of cancer is much higher in one country than in another, rarely say that there is something unique about each of these countries. They begin collecting data about variables which, on the basis of previous research, have been linked to this type of cancer. There may be several characteristics of these countries which make them quite different from one another; but most of them will not be in any way relevant to explaining the nature of the particular phenomena under investigation, whether it be cancer or, in our political science example, the way in which revenue equalization is handled.

In the social and political world, relationships are often more complicated and the boundaries between different variables are not as clear-cut. Nevertheless, there is much to be gained from minimizing differences between systems, selecting countries on the basis of interesting problems and de-emphasizing their unique and different nature. By this means, we can generate common cases from several countries. Since many of the more interesting countries differ radically from Canada in terms of epoch or state of development, I would like to discuss briefly some of the misgivings people may have in transcending these dimensions.

B. Comparisons Across Time

The most frequent comparisons made in the study of Canadian federalism, and Canadian politics generally, involve comparing the present with the past: powers held by the federal government presently are compared with the powers which were held during the second World War; the era of co-operative federalism is compared with the current era of competitive federalism.[3] Many of the comparisons made are not very explicit, and often are used only for descriptive purposes. In many cases, explanations are implied when authors refer to changes in the underpinnings of Canadian federalism. It should also be emphasized that nation-building, province-building and nation-breaking are processes which occur over time. For this reason, if we wish to corroborate our suspicions about what may be unfolding in Canada, it is possible to look at past trends and developments elsewhere. Thus, the creation of the Irish Republic, and the subsequent pattern of relations between Britain and Ireland, may offer lessons as to what relations might be like between a separate Quebec and the rest of Canada.

The time dimension is important in another way. When we think of comparisons, we usually think in terms of contemporary political systems. However, there were political systems in the nineteenth century and earlier in the twentieth whose experiences may well be relevant to understanding the Canadian situation. The case of Ireland and its separation from Britain in 1920 is one obvious example. Less obvious might be the Austro-Hungarian Empire and pre-war Czechoslovakia. In the former, a variety of constitutional arrangements were attempted, including a kind of cultural-linguistic corporatism, which cut across the territorial dimension in order to bind together very diverse societies.[5] The failure of the Austro-Hungarian empire can be traced in part to these elements of diversity; but also important were the demands placed upon the system by certain of the units within the empire. Hungary, for example, dominated by the Magyar community, demanded a special status within the empire. The constitutional compromise of 1867 essentially resulted in a form of dualism within the empire, and this resulted in a great deal of bitterness on the part of the Slavic community (Gordon and Gordon, 1974). It may well contain some useful lessons for those contemplating different means of constitutionalizing dualism within Canada.

Czechoslovakia during the inter-war period was a democratic republic, though not a federal one. Its experience is interesting largely because of the role of the German community in the Sudetenland (Breugel, 1973). In terms of ethnic relations, the country was relatively stable until the mid-nineteen-thirties. Two sets of questions follow: first, what mechanisms (if any) were involved in representing the interests of German-speaking Sudetenlanders in the parliament and bureaucracy, and to what extent did they see the Czech state as being legitimate; second, what factors brought about changes in the relationship shortly before 1938? It could be that the source of instability was primarily from outside Czechoslovakia, and that without the intervention of Germany, the republic would have continued to be viable.

The time dimension, thus, has two aspects. We can compare two systems over time, and compare systems drawn from different historical epochs. Both types of comparison can yield valuable information. The former is a type many people engage in automatically, though not on a very systematic basis, whereas the latter is something many people shy away from. However, if the limiting conditions are properly identified and controlled, the number of cases available for examination will be greatly increased.

C. Comparing Western with Non-Western Systems

During the 1950's and early 1960's, a common theme in the literature on political development was that there was a category of nations which could be called developed and another category of so-called undeveloped nations. The latter referred mainly to the newly emerging nations in Africa and Asia, as well as to the older but still undeveloped nations in South and Central America. Since then, the very distinction between developed and undeveloped nations has come under attack (Milne, 1972). Some analysts have suggested that many traditional elements in so-called undeveloped societies can be considered modern, or at least not incompatible with the modernization process (Bendix, 1967; Rudolph and Rudolph, 1967). Other have stated that there is no clear relationship between the structures of a new state and actual outputs (LaPalombara, 1970).

There are important differences to be sure: third world countries are characterized as having been under colonial rule, being relatively non-aligned, and seeking to industrialize as quickly as possible. They are also seen as having problems in integrating different groups and regions, in providing stable government, and in keeping conflict within manageable bounds. In particular, it is argued that many of these new societies are constantly threatened with incipient civil war as a result of competition between leaders of the different communal groupings; it is claimed that these leaders can find no common ground, perceiving all conflict as a zero-sum game (Rabushka and Sheple, 1972). This is contrasted with the allegedly more moderate politics of the first world. But with the passage of only a few years, this distinction is also being questioned. Communal conflict, often discussed under the rubric of ethnonationalism, has reared its head in a number of the more advanced industrial societies (Esman, 1977). The current conflict in Northern Ireland is just as intractable as many of those in the non-Western world. Nationalist movements having regional bases within nations have sprung up in Britain, France, Italy, Spain, Yugoslavia, and Canada. The black power movement in the United States can also be put in this category, although it lacks a territorial base. In this dimension, therefore, it appears that Western countries share at least certain characteristics with non-Western nations.

What makes ethnic conflict in the third world particularly relevant is that several of these countries adopted federalism as a method of satisfying ethnic group demands for autonomy. Furthermore, over time countries like India and Nigeria have adjusted their federal arrangements to account for new ethnic demands. India re-adjusted state boundaries and created new states in 1956 to ensure as much as possible the internal homogeneity of states in terms of language and ethnicity (Watts, 1966). The aim was to avoid the overlapping of state and linguistic boundaries, which had resulted in linguistic minorities within several of the states, many of whom felt aggrieved by the treatment they received at the hands of majorities. In Nigeria, the problem was how to reduce the dominance of the Northern Hausa ethnic group. This group was essentially bounded by one of the four states; however, it constituted over fifty percent of the population, with the result that the Northern People's Party dominated the central government. The tragedy of civil war over Biafra's attempted secession may be attributed in part to this situation. The military authorities who have ruled Nigeria since the end of the civil war have introduced an administrative system involving 12 states; and the new constitution, to come into effect in 1980, has 19 states. The basic strategy was to fragment the dominance of the largest ethnic group through the creation of individual states, thereby creating a more balanced federal arrangement. Thus, here we have two third world countries employing different strategies to deal with ethnic conflict within federal arrangements. They may well offer lessons for Canada. It would be difficult to slice a province like Ontario into smaller units, or to create units which are internally homogeneous. However, we should be wary of proposals which move in the opposite direction: the creation of a single, cohesive English-Canada, through the reduction of the strength of the English-language provinces, which would dominate French-Canada; or the creation of further linguistic minorities within the different provinces. In this regard, it is worth stressing the case of Pakistan before 1971. Territorial divisions within the Western region of Pakistan were eliminated in 1955, resulting in the creation of a single, politically cohesive province, West Pakistan, which ended up dominating the larger but much poorer province of East Pakistan (Watts, 1966; Sayeed, 1967). With hindsight, one could argue that a more fragmented Western region, consisting of the three original provinces, would have provided additional countervailing forces within the federation and more leverage for East Pakistan.

One objection to Western/non-Western comparisons is that the former colonial status of many of the new nations distinguishes them from the nations belonging to the first world. It is suggested that the process of socio-economic development of ex-colonies was retarded as a result of the dependency inherent in the colonial relationship (Frank, 1969; Furtado, 1967). The dependency thesis has been questioned; nevertheless, much of the political activity taking place within new nations is concerned with removing the remaining vestiges of colonialism. But is this unique to the new world? A recent book by Michael Hechter (1977) entitled *Internal Colonialism*, is concerned with the phenomenon of colonialism inside Great Britain itself. It documents not only the way in which Wales and Scotland were integrated into the national state but also how at an even earlier stage districts such as Northumberland were subdued and integrated into the national state and indigenous cultural elements deliberately eroded by the central authorities. Hechter began his career as a political scientist by first studying the third world. He then

7

discovered that many of the tools and concepts could equally well be applied to a country like Britain. He argues essentially that the current revolt of the Celtic fringe is seen best as a process of decolonization. In Canada, the relationship between Quebec and the rest of Canada is occasionally seen in quasi-colonial terms. In fact, a recent book on the changes in Quebec society has the title *The Decolonization of Quebec* (Milner and Milner, 1973).

As well, descriptions of the relationship between the Canadian west and central Canada (i.e., the manufacturing and financial centres of Ontario and Quebec) often bear a resemblance to the literature on co-lonialism (MacPherson, 1953). This suggests that the experience of new nations may not be so far removed as we think. At a minimum, an examination of third world countries will indicate whether or not it is legitimate to use terms like "quasi-colonial status" in the Canadian context. We can learn other things as well. Of prime importance to many third world countries is rapid economic growth and industrialization. Having the examples of the industrial and post-industrial revolutions before them, the prime goals of virtually all new nations is to speed up the process of economic development as much as possible. A variety of strategies have been developed by the different countries to achieve this goal: five-year plans, emphasis on the rapid development of heavy industry, such as steel plants, the introduction of labour intensive indus-tries, and so on. Unfortunately, many of these strategies have failed to produce results. Their failure, however, may well be illustrative of what can go wrong. Of major concern currently in Canada is regional economic development. In the early post-war period, the emphasis in Canada was on developing the national economy, while scant attention was paid to regional disparities (Smiley, 1976, pp. 128-134). Since the early 1960's, however, serious attempts have been made to disperse economic growth more widely. The strategies employed by both the federal and the provincial governments, as well as a number of the resulting failures, bear some resemblance to the efforts of third world countries (Mathias, 1971). Furthermore, Canada, unlike the United States, Japan, and many West European countries, is highly dependent on foreign investment, branch plants, and the export of raw materials to other countries (Hutcheson, 1978).[6] This places Canada closer to many third world countries.

In comparing third world countries with Canada on the dimension of economic development, one might want to look at the specific strategies employed. Further questions one might want to explore include: to what extent are local governments involved in the planning and development stages? Does the initiative come from the centre or do elites on the periphery play an important role? What effect do federal structures have?

Do they determine the degree of decentralization of patterns of growth? Does the centre attempt to by-pass or co-opt local governments? With regard to the industrialization projects themselves, to what extent are deprived regions exploited by external agents (e.g., multi-nationals) who become involved in such projects? Does the existence of autonomous institutions coinciding with deprived regions lead to competition between regions to the detriment of all concerned?

Many of the new nations have adopted federal systems, and some like India deliberately examined the Canadian case in order to avoid certain of the pitfalls into which the Canadian system had fallen. Now that we are seriously revising our constitution, perhaps it is time for us to look at the newer federations to see whether they, in fact, have avoided our pitfalls. We may well profit from their experiences.

D. Comparing Federal with Non-Federal Systems

The distinction between federal and non-federal systems is not clear-cut. It is very difficult to find a purely federal state which meets all the criteria concerning the independent and co-ordinate status of governments as originally specified by K.C. Wheare (1946). At the same time, it would be unusual to find a system which can be called a purely unitary state. Most polities are decentralized in some form, even if it is only at the administrative level, as in France. Federal arrangements are unique, however, in that they do give institutional expression and a degree of autonomy to territorially-based interests. These territorially-based interests need not be unusually strong, although institutions do tend to render the territorial cleavage more politically salient than might otherwise be the case. Societies like Germany which have a federal arrangement may be quite homogeneous in terms of culture, economic interests, and other matters. On the other hand, societies having a unitary system may be highly pluralistic and fragmented: Belgium is an example. Thus, it should be kept in mind that both federal and non-federal systems can be either homogeneous or pluralistic in their societal make-up.

Under what circumstances do we compare federal with non-federal societies? And what type of non-federal systems do we examine in undertaking comparisons of this sort? Since social science is concerned with the relationships between variables, the only way one can tell if there is a relationship is if there is variation in the variables of interest. Thus, frequently the only way we can evaluate whether or not federalism has an effect on policy-making, for example, is to point to examples which are similar in most respects but are not federal systems. In some instances, therefore, it may well be worthwhile to compare a country like France with Canada. The former is a highly centralized unitary state,

9

while the latter is not. A comparison of this sort can highlight the impact of federalism on economic planning. National economic policy may well be much more coherent in France. But the Canadian political system may be much more responsive when it comes to dealing with local needs than is France. Thus, it is important to look at non-federal systems in order to provide a basis for comparison.

There are also more pragmatic reasons for looking at non-federal systems. In many instances, the kind of examples we are looking for are not in evidence in other federations. Very few federations have linguistic divisions similar to Canada's. Switzerland has three linguistic groupings and the linguistic cleavage is further complicated by the religious cleavage (Steiner, 1974). Yugoslavia, a federal society, has four linguistic groups. Belgium, a unitary state, has two (Lorwin, 1966). In spite of its unitary character − albeit becoming federal − it is similar to Canada in certain respects. One of the interesting aspects of societies with two language groups is that institutional divisions tend to generate more than one minority. Within Canada as a whole, French-Canadians are in a minority. However, within the province of Quebec there is an English-language minority. And one can find significant French-language minorities in the provinces of Ontario and New Brunswick. The interests of these three French-language communities are often contradictory. This makes it difficult to develop language legislation which will meet with the approval of the different minorities. In Belgium as a whole, the two language groups are in relative balance. In Brussels, however, the Flemish are in a distinct minority position. But again the interests of the Flemish community in Brussels are frequently at variance with those of the Flemish living outside of Brussels. In the spring of 1980, the Belgian government fell because proposals for constitutional change, though acceptable to the two main language groups, proved to be unacceptable to the Flemish minority in Brussels. It drives home the point that proposals for constitutional change in countries like Belgium and Canada must take into account the interests of more than one minority, even though these minorities may speak the same language.

Examination of relatively homogeneous unitary systems also has its uses, particularly in the area of constitutional engineering. In the case of West Germany, a new federal constitution, the Basic Law, was imposed on a war-torn society (McWhinney, 1966). This provides us with one example of constitutional engineering in a federal society. However, it is difficult to evaluate in what way the Basic Law has contributed to the stability of post-war German society. A great many other variables, such as economic growth, reactions to the horrors of war, and the experience of a totalitarian regime, may also account for this stability. In France, by contrast, the transition from the Fourth Republic to the Fifth occurred within a very short period of time. In this case, therefore, it is possible to pinpoint with greater certainty the effects of constitutional change. Many of the basic social and economic forces in French society remained constant. The influence of these forces on political life, however, was altered largely because of institutional changes: the legislature in the Fifth Republic became much less important, and many interest groups which previously had access to government through parliamentary deputies found that their influence had declined considerably (Brown, 1968). In terms of learning what might be achieved through constitutional engineering, the French example is instructive.

As noted at the beginning of this section, there are forms of decentralization other than the federal model. It is possible, for example, to decentralize government authority to groups in society which do not have a territorial base. In the Netherlands, for example, socio-religious subcultures have a great deal of autonomy not only in the cultural sphere but also in economic life (Lijphart, 1968). All the major blocs in Dutch society are represented on major decision-making bodies in areas like national economic policy. The socio-religious blocs in the Netherlands, though lacking a territorial base, gained considerably in importance because of changes in the early part of the twentieth century in the manner of disbursing state funds in education, culture, and welfare. One reason for wanting to look at decentralized non-federal systems is to see if they offer a model which we might want to adopt as an example for Canadian political development. It has been argued that in Canada we should try to promote class-based, as opposed to provincially-based, communities (Horowitz, 1968; Porter, 1965) or, alternatively, that we should structure our political institutions on the basis of the two linguistic communities.[7] In all instances, we would want to examine non-federal societies in order to obtain some idea as to what kind of polity would develop if we were to try to encourage the growth of non-territorially-defined communities.

Thus, there are a number of reasons why we should want to look at non-federal societies. They provide us with a basis for comparison and models for Canadian political development. As well, they add to the number of cases available for analysis, particularly in studies of constitutional engineering, non-territorial forms of decentralization, and ethnic/linguistic pluralism.

So far, I have argued that meaningful comparisons can be made between countries which on the surface appear radically different from one another. Some examples were given of the parallels between Canadian and non-Canadian experiences and the lessons which could be drawn from them. Now it is time to move to the substance of this study: the following chapter is concerned with the nature of political communities and the conflicts and issues which can arise between them. The third chapter will discuss some specific proposals for constitutional change and how they would effect political integration in Canada.

11

Footnotes

1. An examination of all the submissions made in the hearings held by the Task Force on Canadian Unity in 1977 and 1978 revealed that virtually no one made reference to the experiences of nations other than Canada. One of the few exceptions was the brief submitted by Gordon Gibson (1977) commending the institutions of Germany and Switzerland as examples Canada might like to follow. The lack of interest in comparative political experience is ironic because in other sectors there is considerable interest in what happens outside of Canada. Canadian businessmen constantly look at developments abroad, and policy-makers in Canadian government (both civil servants and politicians) often use the experiences of other nations when designing policy. In these instances, the charge that outside experiences are irrelevant is heard much less frequently.

2. It should be emphasized that my approach differs from others'. Anthony Birch (1955,1967), for example, argues in favour of a "most similar" approach in doing research in comparative federalism: "My own belief is that the kind of comparative study most likely to be fruitful is that which takes as its starting point the existence of somewhat similar arrangements which have evolved or have been devised in a limited number of countries themselves not entirely dissimilar to meet similar needs." (1967, p. 77).

3. One of the finest examples of this approach is J.R. Mallory's "Five Faces of Federalism" (1965).

4. Not too long ago, it was generally thought that the single-member constituency electoral system in Canada had either the effect of helping to create a two-party brokerage system (Corry and Hodgetts, 1946), or had no effects whatsoever (Meisel, 1963). Cairns (1968) argued that these views were inaccurate and cites the work of Lipset and Duverger with regard to the incentives for sectionalism inherent in the single-member constituency system. Thus, these effects were not unknown previous to Cairns' article, though perhaps not in Canada.

5. In the Austro-Hungarian Empire, there were two experiments with linguistic corporatism in 1897 and 1900, whereby individuals enjoyed government services (primarily education) and privileges in their own language, administered by the "Curia" of their own nationality. Individuals could opt to identify with a national community. If they exercised their option to affiliate, they would be registered on a special list; and instead of voting for the national assembly, they would vote for the Curia of their choice. These experiments were not extended to the whole empire and lasted only a short time: they were last minute efforts to save a crumbling empire. For details, see Robert Kann (1950) and Carl Friedrich (1973). The "Federation des Francophones hors Quebec" has proposed a limited form of linguistic corporatism in Canada. See footnote 7, below.

6. See also Levitt (1970) and Williams (1979). Glen Williams in an interesting analysis has compared the Canadian industrial strategy (the National Policy, high tariffs, etc.) to those pursued by many Latin American countries and many African countries as well. Rather than focussing on developing large-scale export-oriented industries, these countries concentrate on Import Substitution Industrialization (ISI), establishing industries whose goods substitute for imported products in the home markets. Williams argues that Canada can be placed in the ISI category, thereby explaining Canada's industrial backwardness.

7. The "Federation des Francophones hors Quebec" has made proposals to this effect (1979). For example, it would like to see a new upper chamber, the House of the Federation, with equal representation from Anglophones and Francophones.

> "The House of the Federation should be the place where the two founding peoples meet on an equal footing to establish federal policies which reflect the reality of the two founding peoples without regular discussions with them to make sure that its undertakings respect their values and priorities." (pp. 55-56).

Francophone representatives would constitute 50% of this body and be drawn from across Canada. Anglophone representatives, too, would be drawn from across Canada, including Quebec.

2 Cleavages, Institutions and Political Communities

Federal systems usually consist of two or more territorially-based communities co-existing within a larger community. But the nature of these communities can vary. In societies like Australia, the populations of the different states are very similar in terms of language, lifestyle, and culture; they are distinguished primarily in terms of specific historical traditions and constitutionally-defined boundaries. There are other federal societies, however, such as India, where communities are defined more by race, language, or ethnicity. Political institutions may be important but would not be primarily responsible for defining the boundaries of the communities, which are self-evident. But what are the differences between federal systems based on "institutional" communities and those based on "natural" communities? Are the issues which arise between ethnic communities more intractable than those arising between non-ethnic communities? Is the potential for the secession of territories greater when ethnic communities are involved? How do ethnic differences relate to other patterns of cleavage, such as class or regional economic disparities? These are some of the questions explored in this chapter.

Such questions are particularly relevant to the present Canadian debate. The communities in Canada are both sociological and institutional, and there is a lively debate about which aspect is more important. The position one takes greatly influences both the diagnosis of and the prescriptions for resolving the Canadian dilemma.

Several years ago W.S. Livingston (1956) argued that federal systems are largely the product of social forces. Livingston made this argument in response to the older legalistic tradition exemplified by K.C. Wheare (1946), who focused largely on the forms, as opposed to the substance, of federal systems.[1] Academic traditions and modes of analysis wax and wane, however, and in recent years the so-called sociological approach has fallen into disrepute. A writer like William Riker (1964), for example, perceives federalism as a bargain between different geographic entities, the nature of which depends upon the working of the party system. Daniel Elazar has stressed the interdependence of the different units of the federal system. And most recently, Alan Cairns (1977), taking a view directly opposed to that of Livingston, has argued that federal systems are largely the product of institutions and not societies. Livingston, unfortunately, did not develop his sociological approach very far, and, in fact, after his preliminary chapter, he focuses largely on institutions, paying scant attention to social forces.

In this chapter, I will not argue that sociological factors determine federal systems. Rather, I will argue that societal and institutional cleavages interact in complex ways: under certain conditions, the interactions produce distinct regional or group interests which can be used by elites to create cohesive political entities at the subnational level. Furthermore, I will argue, contrary to Cairns, that institutions without a social basis will have no effect on the politics of a federal system, or any system for that matter. Institutions may not be the product of societies but they do need to strike a responsive chord in their societies in order to survive and flourish. They must be attractive to elites as vehicles for promoting their interests as well as those of their constituents. In short, there has to be some sense of community, of a political society, in which leaders, citizens and institutions play a role.

This chapter then, is primarily about the nature of political communities, their relationship to patterns of cleavage, and the kinds of political processes associated with these communities. Of particular importance is the analysis of the variety of conflicts arising between two or more communities within a political system.

Federal systems give territorially-based communities institutional recognition. Other communities are not necessarily based on territory. For example, class-based political communities, although they have never been very sharply defined in Canada, are important elsewhere. One can also have religious communities: in Canada, historically these have provided a basis of support for political parties both national and regional. Another extreme case, the Netherlands, had, until quite recently, well-defined religious subcultures, each with its own political party and social institutions (Lijphart, 1968). Linguistic communities, too, are often politically relevant since they frequently cut across territorial and formal boundaries, as they do in Canada.

The importance of non-territorial political communities lies in part in their role in knitting together or cutting across those communities which are based on territory. One of the major questions involved in constitutional change is what *kinds* of communities will be preserved and developed under each of the different proposals for change (Simeon, 1978). Do we want to maximize the possibilities of class-based politics, a state of affairs favoured by Porter (1965) and Horowitz (1972)? Or do we want to affirm and enhance the political communities defined by provincial boundaries? An understanding of shifting patterns of political cleavage in Canada is important in identifying the rise and decline of various political communities. The critical pressures on the Canadian federal system were largely the product of religious influence and the rise of other forces such as ethnonationalism. For these reasons, this discussion will not be restricted to territorial communities or to those defined in terms of formal boundaries (e.g., provinces). The importance of the following sources of cleavage in structuring and enhancing the development of politically relevant communities will be discussed in sequence: religion, class, ethnicity, territory, and institutions. Examples drawn from several federal and non-federal societies will illustrate how various cleavages can combine to help create distinctive communities.

What follows is a brief discussion of communities and political conflict. This is a prelude to the main discussion of lines of cleavage and the interaction between them.

A. The Nature of Community and the Dimensions of Conflict

What is a political community? The three fundamental elements are: citizens, leaders, and a sense of common purpose. It is quite possible to belong to more than one community, as individuals do in most federal systems. That a community consists of citizens and leaders is to state the obvious: a sense of common purpose, though, is a concept which is both elusive and critical to understanding the linkages between the leaders and the led. For a community to exist, individuals within the community should be aware that they share some sort of collective interest. This collective interest or common purpose may be fostered actively by elites, or elites may merely reflect interests which are very strongly held by citizens at large. Secondly, the community must be willing to use political means, such as supporting a particular party or movement or a specific set of political institutions if it is to be referred to as a political community. Thirdly, a sense of common purpose is linked with one or more lines of cleavage, as communities have collective interests which are distinct from those of other communities. Thus, we can talk about a division or cleavage between the communities of Canada and the United States, between French-Canada and English-Canada, between Protestants and Catholics, and between workers and employers. What separates communities, and to a large extent defines them, is the distinctiveness of the combined interests of citizens of each of the communities in question. Workers have economic and cultural interests which differ from those of employers, but workers must perceive that they share common concerns, if the result is to be collective political action.

Individual interests and demands have definite relationships to patterns of cleavage. Certain interests are fixed and immutable: skin colour, for example, is not a matter of individual choice. Skin colour in and of itself is not necessarily politically relevant, but it frequently serves as a basis for discrimination, positive or negative, and may lead to a collective sense of grievance among those discriminated against. Other cleavages, such as class, may enhance this sense of grievance, but by and large something like race can very easily produce a sense of solidarity with little effort needed from other cleavages, institutions, and leaders. Other characteristics may be more a matter of choice and self-definition. Occupation might be linked with certain interests, but would not necessarily be affixed to the individual for life; a person could become upwardly or downwardly mobile, and as a result become a member of a different community. A Catholic may cease attending mass and no longer see religious values as very important (Lorwin, 1974). Cleavages of this type lack visibility: it is not immediately obvious to which community an individual belongs; and the individual himself may not be sure of his membership. For this reason, institutions and leadership are much more important in defining and maintaining the boundaries of the group and in defining the interests and goals of its membership in instances where distinctive criteria such as race are lacking (Rogowski, 1974).

In the literature on social divisions, a major theme concerns the moderating and splintering effects of cleavages which cut across one another. In general, the notion that cleavages either reinforce or cross-cut one another is too simple and is, in many instances, misleading. Diverse social interests are not always mutually exclusive and can quite often produce a well-defined hybrid. And within territorial units, contradictory class interests are frequently reconciled into a single interest and pitted against those of other territorial units — as in the Maritimes vs. Ontario, or Alberta vs. Quebec.

Leadership is also important. It is tempting to depict political leaders as entrepreneurs constantly seeking power and influence, using their skills to politicize societal divisions and turning institutions to their own advantage. This is the perspective of Schumpeter (1956) and Downs (1963) and, most recently, Alan Cairns (1977). Societal cleavages provide the resources or material with which political elites develop cohesive political subcultures. However, cultural, social, economic, and territorial cleavages provide different kinds of incentives, resources, and tools to political leaders. The resources and means of control made available by a religious cleavage, for example, are quite different from those involving race.[2] These divisions also imply different obstacles which constrain elite behaviour: an English-Canadian can move to another province if he or she is unhappy with the provincial government. On the other hand, a black in South Africa, the United States, or in virtually any country, does not really have this option with regard to membership in the black community.

Whatever the origins of communities, their interests are frequently at odds with those of other communities. Social conflict usually involves incompatible demands made by groups, which in turn represent and mobilize — albeit often in a very distorted way — the interests, demands and expectations of individuals within the groups. The incompatibility of conflicting demands made by communities on opposite sides of a cleavage can vary. A useful way, therefore, to characterize conflicts is to describe them, in the language of game theory, as zero-sum or positive-sum games. The former involve redistributive demands, whereby one side can gain only at the expense of the other; the latter involves distributive demands, whereby all parties concerned are seen as winners (though not necessarily all gaining the same amount). Responses by authorities can be described in similar terms: they can cater to individuals or to groups; they can distribute governmental resources on either a proportional or a disproportional basis (Peters et al, 1977). Generally, demands by groups for redistribution of scarce resources are much more difficult for governments to handle than demands merely calling for proportional distribution (Lijphart 1977a). The really important question becomes: what kinds of social cleavages are more likely to produce redistributive demands? This question has obvious implications for understanding the Canadian experience. It also has implications for developing strategies for change which might enhance the viability of some kinds of communities but not others.

The concepts voluntary and obligatory communities, group interests, and political leadership, direct us to consider the theoretical expectations and empirical realities of inter-community conflict: class, religious, ethnic, territorial, and institutional.

B. The Religious Cleavage

The current debate over the future of Canada is coloured very much by the politics of language, the politics of regionalism, and concern with economic well-being. Religious issues rarely enter the debate. Yet, to understand how federalism operates in Canada, one must assess the religious factor in the historical perspective. The religious cleavage in

Canada was perhaps the dominant line of political conflict in the past, even though it was a moderating force in many instances. Moreover, the relative decline of religion as a factor in the past two decades has probably helped intensify federal-provincial and linguistic conflict in Canada.

The importance of religion in politics is not unique to Canada. Throughout the world, religious differences have caused some of the most virulent forms of conflict. The crusades, the reformation, the early post-reformation period, the civil war in seventeenth-century England, the Swiss civil war in 1847, and the current conflict in Northern Ireland, are all examples of religious conflict involving the breakdown of civil authority and the loss of life. Religious differences have continued to be salient in politics well into this century, albeit in much less dramatic ways. Separate religious parties exist in many West European countries, and in Canada religion is still the best single predictor as to how an individual will vote in an election (Meisel, 1973).

Why is religion such a potent force? Religious beliefs concern the ultimate values of man's existence, his role on earth, his relationship to fellow beings and to God. But religion also concerns temporal power. Much of the conflict in the Western world has involved the Roman Catholic Church, which for a number of centuries sought to dominate substantial areas of secular life, including political life. The rise of Protestantism, in turn, was lined not only with spiritual issues but also with political and economic changes (Ellemers, 1967). In England and Sweden, incumbent rulers found it convenient to declare by fiat that Protestantism would be the official religion of the state. In other parts of Europe, Catholic and Protestant forces clashed on the battlefield. In the Netherlands, the Protestant revolt was part and parcel of the revolt against Spanish rule. In various countries, commercial elites found Protestantism increasingly attractive, allowing them a much greater latitutude in economic activity.

By the early 1800's, religion had lost much of its potent grip on society, and the distinction between Church and State was gradually accepted. The Roman Catholic Church came to terms with the different regimes in Western Europe and elsewhere, to the extent that it tacitly recognized their existence, but there was still the civil war in Switzerland and Bismark's Kulturkampf. The latter was the result of Bismark's deliberate policies, however, rather than any unusual hostility on the part of the Catholic church towards the new German state (Fogarty, 1957). Although no longer dominating the picture, religious issues have continued to play an important role in politics.

It is still difficult to evaluate the importance of the religious factor because religious conflicts continue to involve economic and political factors, and frequently ethnic factors as well. Thus, conflicts which are often labelled religious ones usually involve considerably more than just religion. Walker Connor (1977) writes that the conflict in Northern Ireland is primarily ethnic, with religion playing only a secondary role. However, assuming for the moment that it is possible to find a purely religious conflict, we can ask: what is at stake? Power? Material needs? Spiritual values? One answer might be spiritual values. Religion — whether seen as an opiate or as genuine belief — fulfils an important need in many people, and the need for spiritual comfort is frequently fulfilled by organized religion. It should be stressed, too, that most religious life in Western societies has been organized. Indeed, the creation of a sense of community through organization is a hallmark of most Western religions. Furthermore, a general perception that an organization (or a defined leadership) has the monopoly on the source of salvation gives that organization considerable leverage over individuals. If spiritual well-being is something an individual values highly, then the religious organization is in a good position to exact certain types of behaviour. In the case of the Catholic Church, it can impose sanctions such as the denial of sacraments or excommunication. As Mancur Olson (1965) points out in his *Logic of Collective Action*, individualized incentives and sanctions are the strongest means available for ensuring the loyalty of individuals to the organization.

There are, of course, limits to the extent to which religious values can be used for dominating one's own group. The Catholic Church discovered early on that material concerns were just as important to people as spiritual ones. In the middle ages, the Church played an important welfare function. The role of the church in Quebec in dispensing material services is well-known (Quinn, 1963); less well-known, but no less important, was the same role played by the Church for Irish, Ukranian, Polish, and native Indian groups in Canada.

During the industrial revolutions of the nineteenth century, religious leaders in Germany, Belgium, and the Netherlands, and to a lesser extent in France and Italy, discovered that faith and the threat of spiritual sanctions were insufficient to ensure the loyalty of its communicants. Both Protestant and Catholic social organizations were organized by priests, Protestant pastors, and laymen. By taking an interest in the social welfare of workers, small businessmen, and to some extent employers, religious leaders soon had available an additional means of ensuring the loyalty of followers. Catholic and Protestant workers in many instances did not have to join socialist organizations in order to alleviate their conditions. In many cases, confessional organizations arose only in response to socialist efforts, but confessional trade unions often preceded the socialist ones. For many workers it was safer to remain within the old spiritual framework. Why risk one's spiritual well-being for uncertain material rewards by fleeing to the socialist camp? (Lorwin, 1974). It is worth noting that the Confederation of National Trade Unions (CNTU) in Quebec was a Catholic trade union federation until the early 1960's. In the case of the West European working-class, many workers generally did join and support socialist trade unions and political parties. Nevertheless, confessional organizations also enjoyed considerable success, particularly in Germany, the Netherlands, Belgium, and Switzerland.[3] The prime aim of these organizations, however, was not to wage war on behalf of the workers but to preserve the integrity of spiritual values.

Since the separation of Church and state, when much of the Church's temporal power was stripped away, the Church has been concerned primarily with preserving the well-being of confessional institutions which directly affect core values. In so doing, it was highly dependent upon the secular authorities for help.

In the realm of spiritual values, one of the major aims of both the Catholic Church and Protestant groups, was control over education. In countries like Germany, Belgium, the Netherlands, France, and Canada, the schools issue was a major source of political controversy, but one which was amenable to the politics of gradualism. It has often been seen as an enduring conflict; but in most cases it was resolved, and where it has lingered, it has not led to great political instability and violence. The demand for state support for parochial schools was essentially framed in distributional terms. The demand was basically for the right of access, in proportion to the size of the group, to the largesse of the state devoted to education. In the Netherlands, both Protestants and Catholics demanded the right to operate their own school systems with funds supplied by the state, a right which was fully granted to them in 1917 after previous concessions were made in the 1890's. In Belgium, the schools issue was not settled until 1957. These demands were not for total control over the educational system and, thus, did not imply a wish to impose a totally Catholic or Protestant vision on the rest of society. Rather, they concerned a desire for protection from outside interference. In the words of one Dutch Protestant leader in the nineteenth century, what was wanted was "sovereignty within one's own circle."[4]

In one sense, these conflicts can be seen in zero-sum terms since the secular state lost. On the other hand, no massive redistribution of material resources within the society itself took place, and the authority of the state and the secular elite in economic matters remained unaffected. The dependence of religious leaders on secular authorities in the nineteenth and twentieth centuries, and the limitations imposed upon them by the material interests of their clients, led to the moderation of demands. Referring to confessional organizations at the turn of the century, Lorwin

(1974) noted: "The moderation of early Christian social organizations helped to keep the demands of newly mobilizing groups at levels easily manageable — perhaps too manageable for the system." In the eighteenth and nineteenth centuries in Quebec, the ecclesiastical hierarchy and English elites enjoyed a close and interdependent relationship. Indeed, it was the Catholic trade unions in Quebec which kept strike activity to a minimum (Trudeau, 1974). Currently in Poland there is an uneasy truce between Church and state, with both parties attempting to maintain political and social stability. The organization of clienteles behind religious ideologies — or for that matter any ideology — involves activity on a number of other issues, usually material ones. This often has the effect of transforming the original goal from a position of dominance to one of coexistence.

The Netherlands is an example of a nation where political divisions are based primarily on religion and where political activity has been moderate. The Netherlands also lacks cleavages such as language, race, and region, but it does, like all Western societies, have distinct classes. The effect of the class structure, however, is neutralized because it cuts across the different socio-religious blocs more or less evenly. Because of its relative purity, the Netherlands is worth examining more closely as an illustration of the two points raised earlier, namely, elite dependency and the material interests of clients. A further point to notice is the ability of bloc leaders to co-ordinate the perception of their followers.

According to Arend Lijphart (1975), the politics of moderation in the Netherlands is largely due to the purposeful co-operative actions of bloc Protestant, Catholic, Socialist, and Liberal leaders to bridge deeply-felt cleavages in Dutch society. A basic precondition for this co-operation is control by elites over their followers. The religious blocs in particular have a number of sanctions and institutions which both insulate their followers and cater to their material needs and desires. The Catholic bloc was by far the most cohesive, in the sense that elites are able to control their followers. It had available the hierarchal structure of the Church with its centralized command system, and a willing and able clergy who were in a position to apply sanctions and cater to material needs. One of the most important aspects of the Dutch Catholic bloc was that religious elites, in this case the bishops, were the source of spiritual values and had full control over their dispensation. This gave the bishops considerable scope for defining the boundaries of the Catholic subculture, and for deciding what was appropriate and inappropriate behaviour. The individual Catholic had to look to the Church for his spiritual well-being, and no other guidelines existed for him to distinguish between Catholic and non-Catholic behaviour. Since race and ethnicity were not important, Catholics could not use these criteria as ready-made boundaries (Bakvis,

1978). This enabled the Church to shape the perceptions of its followers. In the absence of straightforward and easily observable criteria, Catholics were more dependent on instruction and information from church leaders. Indeed, Dutch Catholics were told for many years that the Catholic bloc was a minority which was being discriminated against by Dutch society as a whole. At the same time, Catholics were asked to support only Catholic social and political institutions and to leave appropriate action vis-à-vis other blocs in the hands of Catholic elites.

The other blocs (i.e., the Protestants, liberals, and socialists) lacked the Catholic spiritual mechanism of control, but they did have a wide range of socio-economic institutions, such as newspapers, radio stations, recreational societies, and the like. They had, in a sense, positive incentives. Once bloc leaders had captured the loyalties of their followers on the basis of religious (i.e., Protestant and Catholic) or economic interests (i.e., socialist and liberal), the various institutions could be used to co-ordinate the views of bloc members. Thus, elites depended upon a judicious mixture of authoritarian control, using spiritual and material sanctions, and positive incentives by way of providing high quality services which were competitive with those offered by other blocs. Elites were in a good position to dominate the perceptions of followers, but at the same time, they were dependent upon the maintenance and well-being of the political system as a whole. It was the secular elite who had granted the religious blocs the right to separate schools and who had permitted, and to a large extent funded, the development of the extremely wide range of socio-economic institutions which were so important in insulating the clientele of the blocs. As well, religious leaders were aware of the limitations of using purely spiritual issues to mobilize their followers without paying due attention to material interests.

For these reasons, the demands made of the political system by religious groups were collectivist but also moderate, in the sense that they asked for the proportional division of state resources in certain areas, as opposed to the redistribution of these resources. They sought to maintain the values of their groups, but not to impose them on members of other groups. The notion of material interests, however, requires further amplification since it is related to the notion of class and, as mentioned earlier, class divisions in the Netherlands are quite pronounced, viewed both objectively and subjectively (Lijphart, 1975).

Catholic and Protestant leaders played an important role in organizing many of the early trade unions, thereby pre-empting the socialists in many areas. This meant that in many instances the working out of differences between employers and employees took place within the major confessional blocs (Windmuller, 1969). In one sense, class here acts as a cross-cutting cleavage helping to moderate religious conflict. The religious blocs had to cater not only to the religious needs of their clientele but also to their economic interests. If the latter were sufficiently heterogeneous, then the leaders could not afford to take extreme positions on behalf of one part of their constituency. Since conflicting economic interests were reconciled within the blocs, this produced moderate positions on the part of leaders in Cabinet policy-making and debate in parliament. In another sense, however, class differences helped to increase the cohesiveness of blocs, and under some circumstances, increased the potential for more extreme religious demands.

All the religious blocs in the Netherlands form roughly a mirror image of Dutch society; all classes are represented in each of them (Lijphart, 1968). How does this contribute to the cohesiveness of the blocs? To begin with, upward mobility, and the perception of the possibility of becoming upwardly mobile, is an important factor in most modern industrial societies, as well as in many of the third world nations (Sorokin, 1927; Lipset and Bendix, 1964). In blocs with a complete complement of classes, upwardly mobile individuals do not have to move outside their own religious sphere or reject their religious identity in order to move up the occupational ladder.

On the other hand, if the religious group is restricted largely to a single class, then upwardly mobile members of that group may decide to defect to another group despite injunctions or exhortations by their leaders. Keeping in mind that there are no racial or linguistic boundaries demarcating the religious grouping from the rest of society, membership is largely a matter of faith. There would be some conversion costs for the defecting individual but a conversion would not be impossible. If membership in the religious group is seen as a distinct liability by a large number of individuals, then this can lead to large-scale defection and the eventual disintegration of the religious group if the larger society is relatively open. Even if membership in the religion is not considered to be a liability, continual exposure to outside values by individuals having to work outside the boundaries of the group may weaken those individuals' ties to the religion. Thus, the existence of a full range of occupational categories within a religious subculture can be seen as an important factor in preserving the integrity of the subculture, since it provides avenues for upward mobility. Class differences should not be seen *ipso facto* as mitigating the influence of religion.

In modern Western Europe, religion has had a moderating influence on political conflict: in the nineteenth and twentieth centuries, demands by religious groups have tended to be primarily distributional rather than redistributional. This is largely due to the need by leaders of religious blocs to reconcile class interests with their dependence on the resources of the state. At the same time, class differences within religious blocs help to prevent the disintegration of these blocs.

What lessons can we draw from this for Canada? The provinces in Canada differ from the religious blocs in the Netherlands: they are based on territory, not religion. In Canada, with the exception of Quebec, religion has never acted as the basis for the cohesiveness of provincial subcultures. Switzerland is probably the only example of a federal society where territorial claims are based, at least in part, on religious claims (Steiner, 1974). Religion, however, has played a role in Canadian federalism, both in structuring the distribution of powers outlined in the British North America (BNA) Act and, in certain instances, in acting to moderate the demands placed on the federal system.

Various sections of the BNA Act illustrate the importance of the religious question at the time of Confederation. Language rights were entrenched only with regard to the federal Parliament and courts and the provincial legislature in Quebec (Section 133). Religious rights, particularly with regard to education, were given much more attention and involved all the provinces (Section 93, s.s. 1, 2 and 3) (Dawson and Ward, 1970). In the formative phases of French-Canadian nationalism, religious values were more important than language. The ecclesiastical hierarchy in Quebec, along with lay Catholics, saw the province of Quebec as the last bastion of Roman Catholicism in North America and of French Catholicism in the world after 1789. For many clergy, the French language was seen not as something to be valued in and of itself, but rather as a means of protecting the faith. At a minimum, the French language was seen as an integral part of French-Canadian culture, whose most important component was the spiritual dimension. Thus, Henri Bourassa in 1915 noted that the French language bore "the immortal seed of modern Christian civilization." (MacMillan, 1978, p. 12).

French-Canadian culture was largely inward-looking and protective: the elites wanted to keep outside influences at a distance. Largely because of the protective influence of the Church, French-Canadians were discouraged from entering fields such as science and commerce where they would be exposed to secular influences. The educational system in Quebec was an excellent example of the way the Church wished to control the destiny of French-Canadian society (Kwavnick, 1968). The result was a society which made certain types of demands on the larger society: Quebec leaders wanted a minimum of outside interference in religious and cultural matters. Well into the 1950's in their relations with English-Canada — both within and without Quebec — when trade-offs had to be made between religious and economic values, Quebec leaders often opted for the former (Falardeau, 1964). Conflicts did arise over issues which tended to threaten severely the spiritual and cultural well-being of French-Canadians. The conscription crisis in 1917 was a result of French-Canadian resentment at being forced to participate in foreign wars in which they had no material, spiritual, or cultural interest

25

at stake. After all, France is where Catholicism died in 1789. Again, however, the cry was for isolation rather than the restructuring of Canadian federalism.

In its relations with the other provinces and the federal government Quebec remained, if not co-operative, at least quiescent. In fact, in the nineteenth and twentieth century, Quebec and Ontario did join together in asking for greater autonomy vis-à-vis the federal government. But on the whole, Quebec political leaders from Cartier to Duplessis were quite willing to contain their strivings for autonomy within the framework of the constitution (C. Black, 1977).

During the post-war period and through the late 1950's, changes in Canadian society and the economy began to undermine the protective bulwark originally created by Quebec religious and political leaders. The transformation which took place in Quebec during the 1960's, the period of the "Quiet Revolution", coincided with drastic changes in the role of the Church in Quebec. It became more open to secular influences under the impact of Vatican II; there was a drop in clerical manpower, with priests and nuns leaving the Church; and rank and file Catholics were no longer dependent on the Church for guidance. The religious component receded and the cultural-linguistic material elements became more important in a revitalized form of French-Canadian nationalism (Falardeau, 1964).

Kenneth McRae (1974b, p. 243) has noted that since 1960, the pattern of institutional segmentation in Canada "has shifted perceptibly from religion to language." He cites instances of French-speaking Catholic high schools entering the public system as French-language public schools both in Ontario and elsewhere, and of demonimational universities, both Catholic and Protestant, being secularized under governmental and financial pressure. McRae sees this shifting of patterns of segmentation as having distinct political consequences, but these are seen primarily in numerical terms. "While all provinces except Quebec have quite substantial religious minorities, the official language minorities are proportionally small and politically weak in all provinces except Quebec and New Brunswick." (McRae, 1974b, p. 243). The question of numbers is indeed important. It lends credibility to the argument by many in Quebec that since there are relatively few French Canadians outside of Quebec, the federal government bilingualism policies are inappropriate, and therefore Quebec should have full control over language policy within the province.

But the shift is even more important in another sense: the politics of religion is qualitatively different from the politics of language. The demands made by Quebec, and Catholic populations in other provinces, were related to the insulation and protection of core values. They did not

26

involve the wholesale redistribution of power within the Canadian political system. Most religious communities in Canada have been inward-looking, with the exception of the militant jingoism of the Protestant Orangeman's Association. Furthermore, religious conflict was largely concerned with education. It did spill over into other areas, like social welfare, but this mainly concerned the interest of the Church in maintaining control, and not in extending it.[5] Linguistic conflict, on the other hand, has involved not only education but also economics, territory, and other related issues. Demands made by Quebec since the 1960's have been of a redistributive character, as opposed to the more moderate distributive demands of earlier eras.

Religious issues also helped to underpin the Canadian party system, linking together common interests in English and French Canada. Religion is still important in disposing individuals towards one party or the other (Meisel, 1973), but in earlier times religion was much more prominent in terms of stirring the public's conscience and party leaders frequently appealed to religious sentiments. The decline of the party system in integrating the Canadian federation may well be related to the decline of religion as an active political force.

The decline of religion, particularly in the province of Quebec, has helped usher in a new era of federal provincial conflict. The coercive potential of the Church is no longer available in Quebec to help provincial elites obtain a stable basis of electoral support; the conservative orientation of the Church towards maintaining the *status quo* has ceased to be important.

Similarly in the Netherlands, the drastic reorientation of the Catholic Church in the 1960's resulted in a considerable loss of support for what used to be the official Church-sanctioned Catholic political party (Bakvis, forthcoming). Since then, the Dutch party system has been in considerable disarray, with the constant arrival and departure of new political parties. The lack of a stable support base for many of these parties is one basic source of cabinet instability (Wolinetz, 1973). In the Dutch case, however, language did not replace religion as a source of conflict. A more relevant case for comparison is Belgium where, as in Canada, the religious and linguistic cleavages have co-existed for several decades.

In Belgium two linguistic groups, the Flemish and the Walloons, occupy respectively the northern and southern parts of the country, with the exception of the national capital Brussels, where the two groups co-exist within the same geographical region. Belgium is a unitary state which is moving towards a federal model. Linguistic regions have been recognized since 1932 but the laws were not generally enforced (Zolbert, 1975). More importantly, the linguistic regions have not served as the predominant basis for political and social organization. The organizations were, and to a large extent still are, based on the so-called "spiritual" cleavage. There are three basic blocs: Catholic, socialist, and liberal. The latter two are basically anti-clerical. A major issue, not resolved until 1957, was full state support for the parochial school system. Most other organizations, trade unions, employer organizations, recreational societies, etc., are usually affiliated with one of the three blocs. Within these spiritual organizations, there have been tendencies towards federalization − that is to say separate sections for Flanders and Wallonia − particularly within Catholic organizations. Linguistic conflict was never absent, but over the years political leaders of the three main parties were reasonably successful in reconciling linguistic differences within the spiritual subcultures.

During the 1960's, however, linguistic conflict has moved beyond the institutionalized lines of cleavage. It has led to the breakdown of party discipline within the major parties − the Catholic party being the main victim − and to the rise of linguistically-based parties (which existed before, but their strength grew considerably during the 1960's). In Belgium, the language issue was much closer to the surface than it was in Canada. Nevertheless, as in the case of Canada, its rise to prominence is related to the changing nature of the religious cleavage. By the mid-1960's, the question of state support for parochial schools had been settled. The Roman Catholic Church, under the influence of Vatican II, had become more liberal. In Belgium, the religious-ideological cleavage for many years did serve to link together rather diverse interests across linguistic boundaries. The current debate over decentralization of political authority, the distribution of economic benefits, language, and related issues, is based on what most people would refer to as more natural communities. However,the issues seem more intractable and conflict seems more destabilizing.

Overall, the evidence suggests that an understanding of how federalism has operated in Canada in the past must include a proper appreciation of the religious factor. The relative absence of religion as a moderating force in the past two decades has probably contributed towards altering the nature of federal-provincial conflict in Canada. Furthermore, it is important to keep in mind that religious cleavages in the Western world are based primarily on organization. Boundaries between religious groups are in a sense artificial, having been created and maintained by elites through organization. Thus, it is virtually impossible to talk about religious communities without making reference to institutions.

I will turn now to the class cleavage, a cleavage which is not dependent upon institutions for survival but which often requires institutional means if it is to be politically salient.

C. The Class Cleavage

Class has not been salient in Canadian politics. Nevertheless, John Porter (1965) and Gad Horowitz (1963) and others have argued that issues involving language and regional identities are misleading and that class is a more appropriate and natural basis for the formation of political communities. Horowitz suggests that if politics were to be based on class issues, politics would somehow become more "creative". A more thorough-going Marxist would suggest that classes, given the appropriate conditions, form extremely cohesive communities and that conflict between class-based communities might lead to revolution. Unfortunately, examples of political systems where the dominant line of cleavage is class are extremely rare. And in the few cases where class is an important line of cleavage, such as Britain or Sweden, it appears that political conflict is relatively moderate. Furthermore, it is difficult in those countries to point to highly cohesive class-based political communities.

Is it possible for class to act as the basis of a cohesive political community? Cohesion is defined as a situation where a given group or collectivity systematically supports a given set of institutions and its leaders, and where leaders, in turn, can command the loyalties of followers and depend on their support in crucial situations.

Over the years in a variety of countries, several parties have competed for the loyalties of both the workers and those belonging to higher classes: none have been completely successful in capturing the loyalties of a specific class. In Britain, the labour party has never gained more than about 68% of the working-class vote (McKenzie and Silver, 1968). A significant proportion of the working-class has continued to vote for the Conservative party. The same is true in other countries like West Germany and Italy, where conservative or middle-of-the-road Christian parties have managed to attract and retain the loyalties of workers (Linz, 1967; Dogan, 1967). Furthermore, there is often more than a single party appealing to the interests of a particular class. In Sweden, there are three parties competing for the favour of the middle-class. In Germany, during the Weimar period before the war (1919-1933), the Communist party and the Social Democratic party were locked in mortal combat competing for the same clientele (Burnham, 1972). This struggle still exists to some extent in France (Levin, 1970).

Why have working-class parties, for example, not been able to achieve the same degree of cohesion as some of the religious parties? The Catholic party in the Netherlands managed to obtain the support of virtually all Catholics for a period of 50 years. Class, in terms of culture, values, and general distinctiveness — in addition to common economic interests — does appear to offer a natural basis for building a more highly organized form of community. Particularly in Western Europe, one can still point to specific characteristics which distinguish the different classes, such as life-style, speech patterns, popular culture, and related matters (Hamilton, 1965, 1967; Haggart, 1967). Frank Parkin (1967) in discussing mainly the British case, points out that working-class values, though not in themselves radical, are nevertheless antithetical to the dominant values of bourgeois society. What then are the limiting factors on political organization? Precisely because class culture is independent of organization, no party or organization has control over these cultural values, so they cannot be used in a coercive manner. In the case of the Roman Catholic Church, the ecclesiastical hierarchy in any given country has a high degree of control over many of the values directly affecting Catholics. This helps to explain the cohesiveness of the Catholic bloc in a country like the Netherlands. By contrast, a working-class political organization would find it very difficult to tell a worker that he or she is no longer a member of the working-class.

Thus working-class political organizations frequently lack the means of coercion and central control necessary to achieve cohesion. It is only if a class has been thoroughly penetrated by the institutional infrastructure of a central organization that sanctions and incentives on the individual level can be applied with any degree of effectiveness. The pre-war Socialist party in Austria probably came closest to approximating this ideal. It controlled a wide range of institutions offering welfare and recreational services for workers which were generally not available elsewhere (Henig, 1969).

What kinds of organizations and institutions other than political parties do class differences tend to generate? In most democratic societies, trade unions and professional organizations cater to economic interests and have available effective sanctions at the individual level to control the behaviour of members. A worker may lose access to his livelihood if he refuses to pay dues or join the picket line; a physician may be suspended from the practice of medicine if he or she breaks the rules of the medical society. However, it is rare for these sanctions to be used to effect wide-scale mobilization. For one thing, organizations of this type are relatively small and are restricted to certain areas of economic life. Their goals are limited primarily to serving the immediate economic interests of their members. Furthermore, trade unions and professional societies usually depend on government authorities for their legitimacy and for help in enforcing rules such as the closed shop. Organizations of this kind, therefore, rarely embark on a full-scale assault against the status quo.

Trade unions aim at improving the economic position of members on a

30

collective basis but their demands are not necessarily redistributional in nature (Rose and Urwin, 1969). Unions are often quite willing to pass on increased costs to others in order to raise the wages of their members. At the same time, they are not unduly concerned whether the costs are passed on to owners of the factory, to consumers, or to government. At times the demands may indeed be redistributional in intent, but they usually occur on a fairly low level and in particular sectors. Furthermore, this redistribution may well take place within a particular class, for example, one group of workers gaining at the expense of another. In countries with centralized trade unions such as West Germany, Sweden, and the Netherlands, the demands made on employers have been very conservative, usually well within the economic growth rates enjoyed by those countries (Olson, 1976). In these countries, trade unions are even more dependent on the munificence of governmental authorities than in Britain and North America. German, Swedish, and Dutch trade unions have been granted some influence with regard to national economic policy instead of specific rights such as the closed shop. Since large centralized unions are responsible for the economic well-being of several thousand workers working in diverse sectors, trade union leaders are unlikely to pose radical demands because they realize that the membership, or a large proportion of the membership, would probably end up absorbing those costs if the demands were to be granted.

In France and Italy, trade unions have never been integrated into the political system and have been given only limited recognition by it. Trade union federations such as the Confédération Générale du Travail (CGT) and the Confédération Française Démocratique du Travail (CFDT) in France, and the Confederazione General Italiana del Lavaro (CGIL) in Italy, are much more militant than those in the Scandinavian countries (Ross, Weitz, 1975). But their militancy is often of short duration and is frequently about issues like preserving inefficient industries (e.g., steelmaking or coal mining in France) in order to protect jobs. As well, the CGT is frequently at loggerheads with the CFDT, as the CGIL is with the more conservative Confederazione Italiana Sindicato Lavorati (CISL).

In Britain and North America where the closed shop is important, trade unions have contributed to the fragmentation of potentially larger class-based communities. Individuals are often keen to preserve status differences, and differences based on skill and seniority, and to resist levelling tendencies of any kind. Doctors like to maintain their distance from nurses, and nurses like to preserve the difference between themselves and nursing assistants. Unions and professional organizations play a very important role in maintaining and, not infrequently, in enhancing these differences.

Communications difficulties can also hinder the development of class-based political communities. In Canada, members of the different classes are dispersed over a very wide geographic area. If one has minimal contact with fellow workers in other areas, perceptions of common interests are unlikely to arise and bonds of solidarity are unlikely to develop. Geography requires at a minimum a great deal of administrative decentralization, and thus trade unions and class-based political parties find it difficult to develop strong centralized organizations. The Canadian electoral system works against the development of class-based political movements, a point which will be developed further in the section on institutional cleavages. In spite of this, in the 1920's in Canada a class-based political movement did appear, with the Progressives representing the interests of farmers. Many of their spokesmen advocated a group-based system of representation so that both farmers and workers would be able to counter the influence of business and financial interests. However, upon electing a large number of their representatives to Parliament, the Progressives soon discovered that there were serious differences between farmers from the different regions. Generally, it appears that in Canada the interests of members of the same class in one locality may well be in conflict with those in other localities. Furthermore, workers and employers in one area of Canada often see their interests as being closely linked, and yet opposed to those of workers and employers in the same industry but in a different locality.

The existence of a federal system in Canada exacerbates this problem since provincial political leaders, and maybe provincial trade union leaders, have a direct incentive to promote differences of this kind. However, the mere fact of geography would probably still lead to the phenomenon of regional interests predominating over national class differences. In Britain, members of the middle-class, and to a lesser extent workers in areas such as Scotland and Wales, have begun questioning their loyalties to the traditional class-based parties. The ethnic dimension plays an important role, but many of the specific appeals made by both the Scottish and Welsh nationalist parties are based on economics (Rawkins, 1978). As will be shown later, class interests and ethnicity are not necessarily incompatible.

Thus, if Canada and Quebec were to separate and all traces of the federal system were to be removed, this would still not offer a guarantee that class differences would become more important. And if class were to become the predominant force in Canadian political life, then as Richard Rose (1968) has suggested, most political issues would be seen in distributive, rather than redistributive, terms. Furthermore, if the experience of Britain is any example, political conflict of this type is unlikely to be very creative.

D. The Ethnic Cleavage

Ethnicity is one of the more ill-defined and most often used concepts in the social sciences. The term is often employed in situations where it really is not applicable and, conversely, not employed in situations where it should be. For example, the conflict in Northern Ireland is most commonly referred to as a religious conflict, whereas it is probably more ethnic than religious (Connor, 1977). On the other hand, the Netherlands is sometimes referred to as an ethnically-divided society, although for the most part, the people share a common culture and a common language. The dangers in misusing the term are fairly clear. For example, recommendations for conflict-reducing mechanisms, based on an examination of a pseudo-ethnic society, might be applied to genuinely ethnically-divided societies for which they are not appropriate.

Val Lorwin (1974, p. 35) has indicated that there is a clear distinction to be made between subcultures or communities based on ideology, (whether religious or political), and those based on ethnicity:

> Segmented pluralism (i.e. pluralism based on ideology) depends on self definition, and the possibility of individual choice was at the origin of the system. In practice there may be high costs in social pressure or individual trauma, of change; but in principle the individual can change at almost any time − definitely and entirely, or momentarily and partially, by simply reading an opposition newspaper or splitting his vote. The availability of individual alternatives distinguishes the politics of segmented pluralism from those based on the cleavages of caste, communalism, race or even language.

It could be argued that Lorwin draws the distinction too sharply. In the case of ideological subcultures, the costs involved in changing memberships are not only those related to social pressure and psychological trauma. As has been noted, different classes in society tend to develop their own distinctive values and life styles. In Western Europe, the speech patterns and accents of the different classes are quite pronounced, and for individuals, difficult to change. Unless an individual from the working-class, for example, is upwardly mobile from an early age, it would be difficult for him or her suddenly to become a part of the middle-class. Changes within the same class are apparently much easier. For example, a working-class Catholic might decide to drop his affiliation with the Church and join the socialist bloc. In fact, this has occurred in several West European countries.

What distinguishes an ethnic from an ideological community? Clifford Geertz (1963), referring to ethnic communities in the developing world, claims that "primordial bonds" act to hold groups of individuals together. The notion of primordial bonds is rather imprecise, however. Others writing on third-world countries, such as M.G. Smith (1965) on the West Indies and J.S. Furnival (1939) on Indonesia, focus more on characteristics such as race or caste as determinants of communities. These characteristics, acquired through birth rather than by choice, serve to demarcate groups of individuals from one another. Communities such as these often tend to develop their own unique values, rituals, dialects, or languages. These act as unifying symbols and aid in the development of primordial bonds by providing members of the group with a sense of identity. As well, these cultural patterns serve to distinguish even further the different communities, although the essential distinction is based on race or caste. Ronald Rogowski (1974, p. 71) avoids the term "ethnicity" altogether and instead uses the term "stigmata" to refer to racial or caste characteristics: "Any characteristic of a group of persons that is (a) easily identifiable by others in their society and (b) capable of being changed only at high cost if at all, will be called a 'stigma'." Individuals belonging to communities based on such characteristics are members by birth and not by choice. For example, it would be extremely difficult, if not impossible, for a Malay in Malaysia to cease being a Malay and to join the Chinese or Indian community. Language is a stigma, although Rogowski notes that it is more easily eroded than race. Using somewhat different terminology, Karl Deutsch (1975, p. 7) wrote that language acts "as an automatic signalling system, second only to race, in identifying targets for possible privilege or discrimination."

What are the implications of identifiable stigmata for social change and political conflict? Societies with cleavages based on distinctive stigmata are likely to have communities making collective demands over a much broader range of issues. Furthermore, political issues are more likely to be perceived in zero-sum terms than is the case in other societies. Why should this be so? Let us again consider the example of occupational mobility. Members of a readily identifiable group are much more likely to make demands for collective upward mobility — to demand that a range of higher-level occupations be made available to them. If these latter are largely in the hands of some other group, then it is unlikely that the "outsiders" will have much success in gaining access to the valued positions. For an individual to move from one stagmatic group to another would involve considerable cost and might well be impossible: he or she might have to learn a new language, or face discrimination; such a person might well prefer to support collective action with fellow members of his or her own group. For groups with less readily identifiable characteristics, mobility is more likely to occur on an individual basis because the costs involved would be lower. In such cases, demands for collective change are less likely to occur; members of a non-stagmatic bloc can leave quietly, without "voice" and become upwardly mobile (Hirschman, 1970). Members of stigmatic groups, however, seldom have available this "exit option". For them, a viable alternative is using their collective "voice" to achieve upward mobility and access to valued positions.

An important factor in determining whether or not ethnic groups will make collective demands for change is their location within the socioeconomic structure of society. Arend Lijphart (1977b) makes a distinction between horizontal and vertical groups. Horizontal groups coincide with the class structure; for example, American blacks tend to be primarily poor and working-class. By contrast, vertical groups cut across the class structure at right angles. Vertical groups are relatively equal to each other in terms of class, status, and power, whereas horizontal groups have the highest degree of inequality.

According to Lijphart (1977b), horizontal ethnic groups are more likely to come into conflict with one another than are vertical groups because of the latter's greater sense of inequality. It should be pointed out, however, that horizontal ethnic groups will often remain quiescent for long periods of time if they perceive their position to be part of the natural order of things. Furnivall (1939) remarked on this point in his study of segmental pluralism in Indonesia. Members of a horizontal group perceive that they are either not qualified to or not capable of acquiring the necessary skills. On the other hand, if members of such a group feel that they are capable of filling higher level positions, that such positions are interchangeable, and that race, language, or ethnicity is the only bar to access, then there is strong potential for conflict (Rogowski, 1974). This perception is most likely to occur if the horizontal group is in the process of becoming a vertical group. Individuals of such groups see that their own kin are capable of filling high status occupations but that they occupy only a small proportion of them. Indeed, stigmata like race or language emphasize that positions in society are interchangeable and that an imbalance exists.

In Canada, French-Canadians were, and still are, disproportionately represented on the lower rungs of the occupational ladder (Public Service Commission, 1980). At the same time, they have not been entirely absent from higher level positions. During the period of the Quiet Revolution, middle-class French-Canadians began to move into responsible positions in the rapidly expanding public institutions in Quebec (Guindon, 1964), but to many it was obvious that they were still excluded from similar positions in the corporate sphere. The major barrier here was that most corporations in Quebec functioned in English and to many French-Canadians it was manifestly unjust that they should have to acquire competence in English at the possible expense of losing their unique cultural identity. They realized that these factors discouraged many French-Canadians from entering corporations and meant that they would remain under-represented in this important sector of economic life (Morrison, 1970). Hence, the pressure for measures which would ensure that French-Canadians as a collectivity would have full access to these positions. The only measures available, however, were ones which placed the cost burden on the other group, namely the English-Canadians. Such measures are essentially redistributive.

Pressures for change occur when members of a group find themselves cut off from positions of status and economic power to which they previously had access. Anglophones in Montreal are a good example of this. Such individuals may then find it advantageous to reactivate and stress certain aspects of their latent ethnic identity in order to take advantage of economic opportunities. Another instance of this occurred in Britain. Since the late eighteenth century, members of the Scottish middle-class have migrated to the south and generally identified with the English middle-class, particularly with the medical and engineering professions. Subsequently, proportionally fewer Scotsmen were mobile in this way. The discovery of North Sea oil opened up new possibilities, and members of the Scottish middle-class saw considerable advantage in attempting to arrogate as much of the new oil resource as possible for Scotland. In the light of other international experiences, they saw it as a means for opening up new avenues for mobility and personal fulfilment. To this end they reactivated a nationalistic ideology, which prior to that time had remained largely in the realm of folklore (Esman, 1977).

For French-Canadians, the use of collective measures is much more critical since what is at stake is the survival of their distinctive culture and language. By contrast, Scots would still be able to survive within the framework of their own limited institutions without damaging either their economic interests or their cultural identity. They still have ample opportunity for mobility, something which is not really the case for many French-Canadians.

The Scottish example illustrates how groups of individuals can make use of rather weak stigmatic characteristics in order to improve their position. This may also be the case of ethnic groups in Canada which do not belong to either of the two founding peoples, and the dispute over bilingualism and biculturalism has created an increasing awareness of ethnic consciousness among them. The attempts by the Canadian federal government to increase the use of French across the country is viewed with considerable skepticism by many whose language at work is English. In many cases, claims have been made that the language and culture of groups such as the Chinese, Ukranians, Italians, and so on, should receive equal treatment. The Chinese in British Columbia, for example, see themselves as constituting within that province a much larger group than the French-Canadians. Some of these groups have approached provincial governments with their requests. In the province of Saskatchewan, a number of separate school districts have introduced the Ukranian language as a medium of instruction, on the assumption of equal legitimacy with the French language.[6] Thus, the tendency of many English-Canadians has been to try to put language policy into a distributive framework by giving all languages other than English an equal claim to public legitimacy. Unlike French-Canadians, however, their claims seldom extend to demands for language rights at work. For groups like the Ukranians, such a policy would provide opportunities for personal development and fulfilment. On the other hand, if such a policy were systematically pursued, it would place the French-Canadians at a distinct disadvantage, since it assumes that English is the one common language. Unlike Ukrainians, French-Canadians use their language not only as a means of personal fulfilment but also in everyday life. Putting all non-English languages on an equal footing with French would be seen as illegitimate by French-Canadians. Unfortunately, for French-Canada, federal government policy which stresses official bilingualism and multiculturalism and denies the notion of biculturalism (Knopff, 1979) has had the effect of encouraging ethnic groups (largely within English-Canada) to perceive language policy in positive-sum terms, rather than as a means of redressing the balance between English- and French-Canada.

As has been discussed, Lijphart claims that conflict is much less likely to arise between vertical groups than among horizontal ethnic groups. However, even where linguistic or racial communities are relatively in balance, there is still a general tendency to see almost every conceivable issue in zero-sum terms. In this regard, Aristide Zolberg (1977, p. 103) notes:

> Belgian politicians have a propensity for identifying almost any choice as favouring one or the other of the two major communities; once an object is defined as valuable by one side, its opposite becomes valuable to the other, so that an American plane becomes "Flemish" because it is other than French.

Stigmatic characteristics act as an easy target for positive or negative discrimination. Furthermore, it is very difficult to design policies which do not have a built-in bias against one side or the other. In Canada, English-Canadians are apparently less willing to learn the second official language than French-Canadians. The requirement of bilingualism for many top-level civil service positions is therefore seen by many English-Canadians as a policy favouring French-Canadians.

In the case of Belgium, Zolberg notes that Belgian politicians have become expert in transforming "all-or-nothing issues" into ones which can be resolved by allocating to the contending parties shares proportional to their bargaining power. This is an extremely expensive process, however, and in many cases it involves the duplication of government services. Thus, during the debate over the acquisition of new fighter aircraft, one Belgian newspaper commented facetiously, "We'll end up taking the Mirage for the Walloons and the American F-16 for the Flemings. That would be consistent with the Belgian habit of splitting the difference." (quoted in Zolberg, 1977, p. 104).

Feelings of superiority or of grievance (whether real or imagined) are often related to the rigid stands made by political leaders on behalf of their constituents. These are not the only factors, however, which make communities based on stagmata unique. Within racial or linguistic communities, it is very rare that any single authority has control over those characteristics which serve to distinguish one community from the others. Leaders of stigmatic communities, in fact, often find themselves being challenged by counter-elites from within the community. Counter-elites might claim that they can better represent the true interests of the group, arguing that the incumbent leadership has been selling out the interests of the community by being unduly compromising in dealings with other communities. They might even decide to undertake extreme, even violent action on behalf of the group. Furthermore, there is no arbitrary authority which can state that certain individuals are no longer members of the community, that they are for example, no longer French-Canadian, Chinese, or Malayan.

By contrast, in communities where the basis of cohesion is ideology and organization, and where stigmata do not play a role, leaders are often in the position of being able to decide who is a member and who is not, and who will receive goods and services and who will not. This assumes, of course, that the subculture is indeed established, that it has access to resources and that it is well-organized, as is the case with subcultures in the Netherlands. According to Ronald Rogowski (1974), such a subculture will have a better-articulated organizational structure, one that penetrates the life of the individual more thoroughly, than will subcultures with strong stigmatic bases. Given the lack of identifiable criteria, leaders of non-stigmatic communities will have greater ability (and, of course, need) to co-ordinate the perceptions of their followers which, in turn, makes it easier to arrive at compromise solutions with leaders of other groups. As well, since leaders of non-stigmatic blocs can decide on membership, more extreme elements can simply be banished from the group.

In stigmatic communities, leaders are not in the same position to withdraw membership privileges from extreme groups within the community, and moderate elements do not have the choice of leaving quietly. Leaders of stigmatic communities are much more exposed to identifiable pressures, and they are frequently outflanked by counter-elites who take more extreme positions on issues affecting the community. Under different circumstances, that is to say in non-ethnically-divided societies, leaders of subcultures cannot move to a more extreme position without alienating their more moderate support base. However, in ethnically-divided societies it is possible for a leader to take a more extreme position without necessarily endangering his or her more moderate support base. First of all, moderates do not have the option of a quiet exit. Secondly, the demands for redistribution involve both externalizing costs (i.e., imposing costs on those outside of the community) and internalizing benefits as much as possible. Moderate elements within a linguistic or racial community may not see much benefit for themselves in policy statements which ask for drastic redistribution, but neither will they perceive any costs. Thus, they may give tacit support to these more extreme positions or at least not oppose them unduly. Only if policies were to cause general economic upheaval or to involve the community in civil war, would the moderate elements have second thoughts. This means that leaders of stigmatic communities are frequently able to take a more radical position on issues than might otherwise be the case, and often they are forced to do so in order to maximize support.[7] The language legislation by the Parti Québécois in the province of Québec (Bill 101) should be seen in this light. It is redistributional in that it takes away jobs from Anglophones. For the most part, this appeases the more radical elements, but also it appears to have the support of Francophones as a whole in Quebec. And for good reason: for the first time in Canadian history, Francophones in Quebec have the opportunity to enter a wide range of occupations not only in the public but also in the private sector, and to use French as their language at work.

Ethnic conflict can impose considerable strain on political systems and tax to the limit the abilities of political leaders to find solutions acceptable to all parties. Yet ethnic conflict is relatively new in the Western world. Why the sudden upsurge within the last decade? Not only in Canada but also in Belgium, Britain, France, Northern Ireland, Spain, and Yugoslavia, has there been a sudden increase in the vitality of ethnic minorities. What is the explanation? According to Lijphart (1977b):

> It was a result of the decreasing salience of ideological conflict along the horizontal left-right cleavage − and, to a lesser but still significant extent, the declining importance of religious differences − that ethnic conflicts have reemerged in recent years. The ethnic cleavages have long been less salient but more

persistent than these competing cleavages. This explanation means that the wrong question was asked: it should not be Why has ethnic conflict suddenly reappeared?, but, Why has it been dormant for so long? The answer is that it was temporarily displaced by more salient conflicts.

In Western Europe, party systems are still largely based on older cleavages, such as class and religion, even though the underpinnings have altered considerably over the years. These institutionalized cleavages help to mute ethnic conflict to some extent. This is certainly the case in Belgium. In Canada, however, the party system, the electoral system, and the provisions of the BNA Act, all have a slight bias in promoting ethnic conflict. The electoral system, at both the federal and provincial levels can help promote the very rapid rise of new parties if the support base is distributed in such a way as to ensure pluralities in several constituencies (Cairns 1968). Provincial boundaries tend to coincide with one of the two founding groups, but at the same time ensure that significant minorities (both French and English) remain in all provinces so as to make the conflict more intractable. The national party system has helped mute conflict of this type in the past, but it no longer appears to do so (Smiley, 1976).

Ethnic conflict has obvious implications for the operation of federal systems. The leaders of ethnic communities are in an entirely different situation than leaders of other types of communities; their ability to reach compromise positions with other leaders is seriously affected by the pressures they face from their clientele. In general, issues are more likely to be construed as zero-sum situations; actual inequalities are more likely to become apparent to the members of ethnic communities. Whether federalism is conceived as a bargain maintained through the operation of the party system (Riker, 1969), or as a system of interdependent units (Elazar, 1962), or as a system of conflict and co-operation between provincial elites (Simeon, 1972), the presence or absence of ethnic communities coincident with federal units can have a drastic effect on the resources, bargaining strategies, and policy stances of the major actors as they try to resolve their differences.

E. The Territorial Cleavage

In recent years, social scientists have rediscovered the importance of territory as a factor in political conflict. It should be noted that conflict between different communities quite frequently involves a territorial dimension even if territory itself is not a salient issue. In fact, it is often difficult to find examples of conflict involving ethnic communities where the territorial factor is entirely absent. Exceptions are Malaysia and Indonesia, where members of the different communities are largely intermingled. But even in Malaysia, the Malays are overwhelmingly predominant in the rural north-eastern and north-western areas of the peninsula. Where there is a mixture of races, as in urban areas, the communities tend to be segregated in different neighbourhoods (Watts, 1966). In the Netherlands, the territorial dimension has never been politically salient, but, even there, territory has played a role. The southern part of the Netherlands contains 40 percent of all Catholics, and 95 percent of the population in that area is Catholic. This homogeneity facilitated the establishment of confessional organizations in the early part of the twentieth century. The viability of class-based communities is considerably enhanced when members of one class are concentrated in a specific geographic area; coal mining and fishing districts are two examples which come to mind (Kerr and Siegel, 1964). What is new, however, is that in recent years territory has become much more salient as an object for popular political discourse.

Geography and the sense of region has always been topical for most Canadians, but elsewhere this has not been so. According to Sidney Tarrow (1978), the industrial revolution in Western Europe led to the predominance of functional interests over territorial interests. In liberal democracies, representation to parliament has usually been on a territorial basis. Increasingly, this was transformed into a channel for functional interests. Labour, big business, small business, as well as religious interests, cut across the territorial dimension. The party systems of the different West European countries effectively "organized in" functional issues and "organized out" territorial issues.

According to Tarrow (1978), Shonfeld (1965), and others, the process of modernization in the twentieth century eroded territorial representation even further. A shift occurred away from parliamentary representation *per se*, and towards "corporatist" representation in fields such as economic planning. Parliament went into decline, and the work of the individual parliamentarian was made irrelevant. Local units, whether municipalities, states, or provinces, became less able to take initiatives regarding policy preferences of local inhabitants. Demands were forced upwards to higher levels where they were dealt with by technocratic elites. Thus Samuel Beer writes:

> In the United States, as in other modernizing societies, the general historical record has spelled centralization. While in recent years a new phase of this centralizing process has set in − which I call technocratic federalism − the main reasons for this change are not to be found in the personal, partisan or

41

ideological preferences of office holders, but in the new forces produced by an advanced modernity. (Quoted in Tarrow, 1978).

In recent years, however, there have been pressures for decentralization, and the territorial unit is often seen as the natural basis for the devolution of political and administrative authority. This development has occurred not only in societies with ethnic concentrations, but also in societies where ethnicity is not usually considered to be an important political factor. Within countries like Austria, Italy, Japan, and the United States, there have been increasing pressures for decentralization.

It could well be that, as in the case of ethnicity, the territorial cleavage, long suppressed by other cleavages, is coming to the forefront now that the underpinnings of the so-called "functional cleavages" have weakened. In modern industrial societies, with their increasingly complex class structures, class distinctions have become less clear. The labour movement, having been integrated effectively into the mainstream of political life in a number of countries, is no longer as interested in class conflict. Religion as a force has declined. But what makes territory attractive as a basis for political activity?

Territory, in contrast to class, offers an excellent basis for political entrepreneurship and, as in the case of ethnicity, a simple and straightforward criterion for discriminating, positively or negatively, against a bloc of individuals. It has been suggested that the very geographical features of a given area will generate particular patterns of culture or result in the predominance of a certain kind of personality; or, alternatively, that long standing traditions of a people have become irrevocably linked with a specific territorial unit (e.g., Palestine and the Jews). However, in countries with relatively short histories such as Canada and Australia, it is difficult to use interpretations of this type to explain the viability of territorial politics.

In Canada and Australia proximity is probably a more important factor. Constitutional provisions aside, local leaders usually have a better sense of existing conditions, and local preferences and grievances by virtue of residency, than do federal leaders. In many instances, local leaders are in a position to develop personal relationships with constituents which they can use in a variety of ways. They can act as intermediaries between central authorities and local citizens, thus helping to integrate the periphery and the centre (Tarrow, 1976). Alternatively, local leaders may find it to their advantage to make demands upon the centre in the name of the territorial community, and others may wish to divorce themselves from central government policies to avoid being cut off from their community. Some local leaders might see co-operation with the centre as a means of upward mobility. However, if there is a surfeit of potential leaders from the peripheries, channels for mobility may become blocked, and local elites may decide to concentrate on developing their local area as a basis of influence. Recently, in the United States, Canada, and elsewhere, local units have acquired their own technocratic experts largely because of the surplus of technocrats on the market, individuals who otherwise may have found jobs with the centre. This has led to the development of technocracies at the local level.

The centre, in turn, is often unable to develop either the administrative or the political structures necessary to ensure the representation of the complete range of interests in the society and to keep abreast of local developments. The failure of political parties in Canada to perform this function is one outstanding example, and this failure may well be due to the reasons cited above. Local leaders are more likely to be better in-formed about local conditions and, if they have the resources, are in an excellent position to outbid the centre for the loyalties of citizens in various policy fields. These loyalties can be seen in largely instrumental terms. There may be other loyalties which are less instrumental, such as deep affection for the terrain or the people of a given area, and these may also be more enduring. These kinds of loyalties are not necessarily translated into loyalty to local leaders or to local institutions. And in newer nations, like Canada or Australia, loyalties such as these may not have had enough time to develop. Instrumental loyalties, however, may by themselves tend towards the development of institutions and may prove to be enduring if elites consistently succeed in delivering valued goods and services.

Proximity permits provincial elites to pre-empt federal leadership on a whole range of policy matters. The size and nature of the market also has an effect. The federal government, if it seeks to act as a broker of regional interests, has to arrive at a common denominator of policy preferences which may not really satisfy anyone. It is much easier for local authorities to arrive at a policy in keeping with the preferences of citizens if they have the resources to do so. Therefore, in Canada, provincial govern-ments may appear to citizens to be attentive, while the federal govern-ment appears to be remote. Furthermore, it is quite possible that citizens may concede in principle that, for reasons of efficiency and rationaliza-tion, the federal government should take a pre-eminent role in certain fields. In particular situations, however, they may well opt for their provincial governments because: a) the provincial government moved on the issue much more quickly because there were fewer internal conflicts to resolve; and b) the individual can see a distinct benefit in having a particular area under provincial jurisdiction, even though it would be at the expense of the nation as a whole (i.e., benefits would accrue solely to citizens of the province, and diseconomies and costs would be borne by the other provinces). Canadians may agree in principle that further decentralization is undesirable and that they see no contradiction between being loyal provincial citizens as well as loyal Canadians. However, in particular situations, when forced to make a choice, the citizen may well opt for the provincial government.[8]

Under what circumstances can conflict arise between territorially-defined units? Conflict or pressures for change can occur when there is a perception that a particular segment of the population is being favoured at the expense of another segment. Such a perception is most likely if the segment in question is clearly distinguishable from the other segments or from the society as a whole. If members of the segment being discriminated against are black, for example, while the society as a whole is white, then the fact of discrimination will be readily apparent. In the case of class, it is often difficult to perceive how benefits are being distributed among the different occupational categories and whether one class is being exploited by another. Information is frequently lacking. Indirectly, class may be a very important determinant of how benefits are distributed, but this is not easily perceived. Classes are not usually treated as distinct collective entities by governments. Territory, however, frequently is used as a basic unit for purposes of administration, regulation and distribution, even in unitary societies.

When one territorial unit is singled out for attention, it is often readily apparent both within and without the unit.[9] Furthermore, the nature of government policy, public goods, and economic development is that its effects are rarely distributed evenly across geographical space. Thus, the politics of territory is often seen in zero-sum terms. The location of a new factory is seen as a gain for one territorial unit and a loss for others. This is true in both Western and non-Western societies (Mathias, 1971).

In a racially divided society, where the races are intermingled, it is sometimes possible to ensure proportional distribution of goods through regulatory means. This is much more difficult to achieve in the case of territorial units. And when it is attempted it usually involves a great deal of expense. Instead of having one large centrally-located steel plant, a country may decide to have several small and inefficient ones in order to reduce feelings of discrimination among the different territorial units. The introduction of miniature versions of the national economy in different areas of the nation might result in the creation of what Lijphart (1977b) calls vertical groups having a geographic basis. This might reduce tensions but the relative independence of these areas can also lead to separation, beggar thy neighbour policies, and the like, since the units may no longer perceive any common interest.

The concentration of a population within a territorial unit promotes the development of communication networks. Thus, unlike the situation with classes which are dispersed across a vast geographical expanse, information concerning discriminatory treatment of a geographical area is much more easily transmitted. This, combined with the ease with which a territorial unit becomes an object for positive or negative treatment, makes it easy for a sense of collective grievance to arise. Although the affective bonds holding the community together may be weak, these other factors can act as a basis for organized political activity.

No discussion of territory is complete without mention of the metropolitan-hinterland or centre-periphery thesis, as originally developed by writers like Harold Innis (1950). There are several variations on the centre-periphery theme. Some writers see the relationship between the centre and the periphery in terms of imperial domination, while others see it more in terms of an equal exchange. Essentially, however, it is seen as an economic relationship whereby outlying areas specialize in the production or extraction of particular products which are then shipped to the centre, where they undergo further processing or marketing. It is a relationship which inherently has a high potential for conflict. C.B. MacPherson (1953) did not make explicit use of the metropolis-hinterland thesis in his analysis of Social Credit in Alberta, but he did discuss the revolt of small commodity producers (i.e., farmers) against eastern bankers and merchants who controlled the flow of credit and means of transportation.

Centre-periphery conflict has been clearly linked by many analysts to regionalization within Canada. Furthermore, it is often seen as an exploitative relationship, with one side (usually the hinterland) losing and the other gaining, leading to the exacerbation of political conflict (Weller, 1977). Centre-periphery conflict does have its limits, however. It can be argued that centre-periphery relationships can help integrate different regions, and that moves to reduce interdependence can, by contrast, have disintegrative consequences. Centre-periphery conflict shares some of the characteristics of class conflict, which make this type of conflict potentially less damaging than, for example, the ethnic variety. Conflict between specialized groups of producers and merchants can be seen more easily as a positive-sum situation, in which it is often difficult to perceive whether one side is gaining or losing. It is similar to the problem of inter-personal comparisons of utility in the economics literature: when two individuals exchange goods, it is frequently impossible to tell whether one obtains greater value or satisfaction out of the exchange than the other (Sen, 1973). In the long run, a centre-periphery relationship may show that the centre has grown considerably more in terms of GNP or per capita income, but this does not necessarily mean that the relationship *per se* is responsible for the outcome. And in other situations, the relationship can be seen by both parties as being symbiotic: the primary producers in the periphery may find that the deck is stacked in their favour. Natural resources like oil or natural gas may be very much in demand and, as a result, the peripheral region in question may be in a position to demand a very high price. Interdependence between centre and periphery may lead to an imbalance in favour of one or the other: the periphery, indeed, may feel frustrated and alienated. However, as in the case of class conflict, there may be very few options available to the aggrieved area, such as alternative markets or sources of raw materials.

Territorial distinctiveness provides the opportunity for a segment of the population to separate from the nation-state and this possibility sharply distinguishes the politics of territory from other kinds. Separation, however, is not necessarily a foregone conclusion, and it is possible to specify some of the aspects of centre-periphery relationships which either promote or mitigate the potential for separation. If the people residing in a given territory perceive themselves to be a complete society, separation is more likely to occur. This perception can arise if the area is relatively independent of other areas. In other words, if the area possesses its own secondary processing industries and is not entirely dependent on other areas for markets or has access to a variety of markets, then it is likely to see the services and goods provided by the centre or other areas within the nation-state as being less than absolutely necessary.

There are some sovereign nations which are highly dependent on other nations for either raw materials or markets, or both, and whose economies are highly skewed towards one particular specialization. Examples might be Japan, the Netherlands, and Canada in its relationship with the United States. These nations, however, possessed distinct identities prior to the onset of industrialization in the latter part of the nineteenth century. Furthermore, countries like Japan and the Netherlands depend on a number of different sources for both their materials and markets.

Matters are often different for a territorial unit contemplating secession which is already part of a sovereign nation. It may find itself landlocked and thereby denied essential services and markets. In Czechoslovakia in the inter-war period, most secondary industries were located in Sudetenland and owned by German-speaking Sudetens. Ethnic links made them closer to both Austria and Germany, and union with either of these two nations was considered a viable option. Self-determination was also considered. However, the Czechoslovakian hinterland, occupied largely by Czechs and Magyars, was the major outlet for finished products, as well as the supplier of a number of the necessary raw materials. According to the historian J.W. Breugel (1973), this was the major reason why German industrialists in Sudetenland supported the regime in Prague. The German Social Democratic Party in Sudetenland tacitly supported the regime as well. There is a strong parallel between the Czechoslovak case as outlined here and Quebec. The latter, as it examines the various options available, may come to similar conclusions concerning relations with the other regions of Canada. Thus, for a centre-periphery relationship to have an integrative effect, there has to be some degree of mutual satisfaction. At a minimum, there has to be a perception of lack of options such as markets in other nations.

Increasing interdependence between two or more sovereign states does not necessarily lead to the merger of these units or even to a federation. Institutions, nationalistic sentiment, and other forces may be too strong to be overcome by integrative forces stemming from economic interdependence. The European Economic Community is a case in point. The lack of economic interdependence, however, is inimicable to the development of *any* kind of political integration. Ronald Watts (1966) cites the absence of complementary economies as one of the reasons for the failure of the West Indies to federate.[10] In Canada, it is argued that one of the stumbling blocks to the union of the four Maritime provinces is the fact that the economies of these provinces are in competition with one another and not complementary (Careless, 1977). Thus, the nature of economic relations between the different units of a federal system is a crucial determinant of the viability of that system.

The existence of different classes within a territorial unit would not necessarily act as a cross-cutting cleavage helping to integrate geographic units, since conflicting classes often look to regional authorities for help in resolving their disputes. The interests of employers and employees are often seen as being complementary, resulting in a perceived common interest, which stands in contrast to that of another region. The politics of industrial location is illustrative of how regional elites can mobilize the support of both management and labour in obtaining new plants for their locality, often at the expense of other regions. Finally, just as in the case of ethnic and religious blocs, class differences can add to the vitality of regional societies.

The lack of interdependence can help in the development of distinctive regional identities. Ethnicity, however, would be the factor which would be most likely to enhance the vitality and unique identity of a given region. Phillip Rawkins (1970), citing the findings of the British Royal Commission on the Constitution, has noted the similarity in attitudes in both Scotland and the north of England. In both regions, the sense of relative deprivation is at an equally high level. However:

The voters of northern England, unlike those of Scotland and Wales, lack a core ethnic identity to form a focus for mobilization against the center. In the absence of historical traces of a consciousness of ethnic distinctiveness, they have nowhere else to go. (Rawkins, 1978).

Ethnicity can be used as a tool by the people of a region to express their discontent against the centre. It can also heighten the sensitivity of individuals to outside discrimination. Ethnic identity and territory can combine to form the basis for nationalist sentiment. In fact, it is rare to have expressions of ethnonationalist sentiments without some reference to territory. South Moluccan terrorists in the Netherlands wish to be reunited with their homeland, although they have never laid eyes upon the islands in question. Ethnonationalism is one of the most potent forces in existence, and one of the most difficult to control in terms of conflict management. Demands are invariably redistributive. Ethnic conflicts may well be superseded temporarily by class or religious conflicts but, particularly if they have a territorial base, they rarely disappear.

There is a further factor which can help enhance the salience of regional issues: institutions. In Scotland, identity was kept alive in part because in 1707 the English granted the Scots the right to retain many of their unique institutions. And in Canada, it has been argued that many of the provinces owe their existence to institutions rather than to indigenous factors.

F. Institutions As Bases of Cleavage

In previous sections it was suggested that institutions, formal and informal, play an important role in shaping the identities of communities. How are institutional factors important? According to E.E. Schattschneider's classical formulation, institutions represent a "mobilization of bias":

> All forms of political organization have a bias in favour of the exploitation of some kinds of conflict and the suppression of others because organization is the mobilization of bias. Some issues are organized into politics while others are organized out. (Schattschneider, 1959).

Thus, the interests of some groups are rendered salient, while others are repressed. In the past, writers frequently emphasized the dependent status of institutions, arguing that they are largely a function of underlying social and economic realities (e.g., Livingston, 1956). In more recent

48

years, there has been considerable criticism of this so-called sociological reductionism. Picking up on the theme of institutions as the mobilization of bias, many researchers have focused on the effects of institutions (such as electoral systems, parliamentary systems and the like) on political life.

In a recent article, Alan Cairns (1977), has gone as far as to argue that "federalism, at least in the Canadian case, is a function not of societies but of the constitution, and more importantly of the governments that work the constitution." According to Cairns, the basis for a federal society in Canada is not the existence of different ethnic, linguistic or even territorial groups, but a constitution which has provided political entrepreneurs with the tools for seeking and obtaining power.

The BNA Act of 1867 undoubtedly provided provincial elites with considerable resources and, in the case of the English-language provinces, probably with their basic identities as well. The decision in 1905 to create the two separate provinces of Alberta and Saskatchewan provided the basis for the development of two distinct provincial units. Several examples can be given of the moulding effect of institutions and constitutions. In Australia during the 1930's, it was common practice to predict the early demise of state governments and their institutions (Greenwood, 1976). This did not occur, and for many people it is an indication of the robustness of institutional structures. The Basic Law in West Germany is seen as an example of constitutional engineering, whereby the direction and nature of the society and its politics was drastically altered (Spiro, 1967). The advent of the Fifth Republic in France brought in not only De Gaulle but also a restructuring of the relationships between the executive and parliamentarians, with the result that many pressure groups which previously had access to government through the legislature found their influence considerably reduced (Wahl, 1967).

However, there is a danger of ascribing too much influence to institutions. I will qualify Schattschneider's famous dictum by arguing that the inherent bias frequently found in institutions must correspond with the interests of at least one of the parties involved in any given conflict. If the institutions do not strike a responsive chord among at least certain individuals or groups, then they may well end up being ignored, thereby having no moulding effect whatsoever. Institutions have an effect only when they interact with sociological forces.

In Canada, the BNA Act originally presented quite a different mobilization of bias than towards decentralization. It presented a bias in favour of the centre. The constitutional provisions framed by the Fathers of Confederation were intended to provide a highly centralized form of federalism. However, after little more than two decades, the centralist

49

bias of the BNA Act no longer had a pronounced effect. From the latter part of the nineteenth century onwards, the centre increasingly failed to mobilize other sources of strength in order to promote and ensure the effectiveness of the constitutional provisions favouring central government control. Instead, many economic and social interests turned to provincial governments for support or protection. These interests and provincial governments were successful in finding provisions in the BNA Act which were biased in their favour. Many economic interests were also important in helping to finance expensive litigation in the courts, in many cases pushing their arguments to the level of the Judicial Committee of the Privy Council. Cairns (1971) has noted elsewhere that the Judicial Committee of the Privy Council (JCPC), in rendering decisions favourable to the provinces, was responding in part to broad scale sociological forces which happened to be regionally based.

The rapid growth in the size and power of provincial governments in Canada was due in part to political entrepreneurship in combination with specific constitutional tools which were available. This growth also was due in part to basic social and economic forces, forces which resulted in demands for the rapid expansion of social and educational services. These trends were unforeseen in 1867; they resulted, however, in opportunities for provincial leaders to fill a need which was under their jurisdiction. Thus, an interpretation of the growth of provincial powers has to take into account constitutional provisions, socio-economic forces, and leadership.

Cairns (1977) states that the post-Confederation history of Canadian federalism is little more than the record of the efforts of governing elites to pyramid their resources. It should be noted that these efforts did not always directly translate into government growth; not all provincial governments sought to maximize provincial growth and expansion. During the 1930's, provincial leaders strongly resisted federal encroachments (E. Black, 1975). At the same time, they rejected opportunities for increasing the scope of their own activities. Most were hidebound by outdated ideologies, which stressed the least amount of government possible. It was not until the post-war period that provincial governments began expanding their bureaucracies, a trend which did not really begin in certain provinces, like British Columbia, until well into the 1960's. The Saskatchewan government from 1944 to 1964 favoured an expanded role for the federal government rather than for the provincial governments, and resisted tendencies toward decentralization (E. Black, 1975). The recently-elected Progressive Conservative government in Manitoba appears to have adopted some of the earlier pre-war notions concerning the scope of government activities and is actively resisting opportunities for further growth.

It is the goal of most governments to be re-elected. In pursuing this goal, provincial governments must often respond to conflicting demands inherent in even relatively undifferentiated economies and societies. This fact helps explain the growth of provincial governments in a number of ways. When giving in to one sector of the population, other sectors often demand equal treatment. Thus, much of the growth of provincial governments may not be due so much to purposeful design as to a perception by provincial leaders that they have no choice but to respond to various claims on governmental resources (Bird, 1970). An important aspect of this is pressure from central governments and competition from other provinces.

During the co-operative federalism phase in Canada in the early post-war period, when the federal government took the initiative in many areas through the use of fifty-cent-dollars and other means (Carter, 1971; Smiley, 1976), provincial governments expanded not unwillingly perhaps, but certainly not on their own initiative. As well, the introduction of particular programmes (e.g., government automobile insurance) in certain provinces often has a demonstration effect: there will be pressures in other provinces for governments to provide similar services (Noel, 1976). Provinces are frequently in competition with one another for capital investment, offering tax concessions and other inducements (Mathias, 1971; Careless, 1977). As provincial leaders expand the scope of their activities, in part to maintain the loyalty of their citizens, they thereby increase their responsibilities. If they make claims at election time to improve the provincial economy, then they may well feel impelled to increase their capacities in the areas of economic planning and related areas. The reasons for the permanence and growth of the different levels of government are many, and it would be false to attribute their growth solely to the innate drives of the governments themselves.

The above interpretation rests in part on some of the assumptions made by students working in the public choice field (e.g., Buchanan and Tullock, 1962). However, it diverges from the public choice literature in several respects: Mark Sproule-Jones (1975), an adherent of the public choice school, argues that the size and nature of the different levels of government is a function of market forces;[11] citizen preferences determine which level of government performs what particular function; governments are like firms which operate according to the dictates of the market. Sproule-Jones sees a positive benefit in overlapping jurisidictions, in that this allows consumer-citizens to choose the package which best meets their needs in the most efficient and economical fashion. The utility of the public-choice approach is that it emphasizes the market aspects of federal and provincial public policy. However, the approach is misleading in suggesting that various criteria of efficiency are being met.

Competition between the different levels of government frequently leads to over-servicing. Consumer-citizens may obtain short-term advantages through competition of this sort, but may suffer longer-term consequences, such as higher taxes, an increase in the public debt,and so on (Rogowski, 1978).

When governments are pressured to undertake programs, these pressures are often the result of political competition within the unit (e.g., a province) or without. And where there are specific demands placed upon them, governments usually have several options available as to how these demands are to be met. What the public choice approach does suggest is that secondary governments operating in the same fields as the federal government generally will be able to formulate policies which are more likely to meet with the approval, and perhaps the support, of citizens in their particular unit than the policies of the central government (Ostrom, 1974). As noted earlier in the discussion of territory, this is in part a function of proximity, but equally important is the fact that provincial governments attend a much smaller population than the federal. Therefore, if the province has a legislative competence in a given area, financial resources, a modicum of expertise, and the political will, it will be in a better position to formulate policies which are in tune with the predilections of that section of the population. Even if it lacks both the legislative competence and the financial resources, a provincial government may still try to obtain the support of citizens in order to press the concerns and claims of the province as a whole. The rise of the Progressive and the Social Credit movements in Alberta is a good example of this (MacPherson, 1953; Mallory, 1954). As well, economic inequalities between regions become more visible when they are given institutional expression. Provincial leaders of "have-not" provinces can then use these inequalities as leverage for extracting concessions from other provinces or the central government. By endowing the provinces with legislative competence in specific areas, provincial governments were given an important boost to their growth and development. But the important point to remember is that these institutional endowments struck a responsive chord in their environment. It was through interaction with social and economic forces that provincial governments developed and took on a distinctive institutional form. This implies that in many ways institutions are largely instruments used by different elites to their own advantage.

Are there circumstances when institutions do have a truly independent effect? That is to say, when they take individuals and societies in directions which were completely unanticipated by anyone? Institutions probably have the greatest influence where there is ambiguity. Citizens of British North America accepted British parliamentary institutions and means of representation, unaware of many of the consequences. It is only recently that evidence has come to light of the manner in which the electoral system has exacerbated regional differences and encouraged certain types of campaign strategies by political parties (Cairns, 1968). There was no intention by anyone, least of all the Fathers of Confederation, that the electoral system should have this effect. And many political leaders are probably still unaware of certain effects of the electoral system. Influenced by British traditions, many leaders in 1867 felt comfortable with British institutions, and in Quebec it was felt that there really was no credible alternative. Most accepted the Westminster model in the belief that it certainly would not harm their interests. Thus, in many instances individuals allow themselves to be guided by rules and institutions for want of anything better, and not because they desire to reach specific objectives.

Institutions set up to deal with particular problems can help resolve similar disputes which arise later. This can have unintended consequences by reinforcing the development of certain kinds of interests. In the Netherlands, demands for control over education by the Protestant and Catholic blocs resulted in an agreement referred to as the Pacification. It represented a resolution of two conflicts, the parochial schools issue and the extension of the franchise. Religious blocs were given access to the resources of the state for the funding of parochial schools on a proportional basis, and an electoral system based on proportional representation was introduced. Thereafter, however, the Pacification and the rule of proportionality exerted influence in other areas. As radio broadcasting developed, it was decided to allocate broadcasting time and facilities on a proportional basis. The same occurred in health and welfare, and cultural life generally. In 1917, the possibility of extending the rule of proportionality to other areas certainly was not widely contemplated, yet over the years, the Pacification has continued to act as a kind of template for the resolution of subsequent issues. It was of considerable importance in aiding the development of cohesive and well-defined subcultures and it allowed subcultural elites to penetrate more thoroughly the lives of individuals, thereby enhancing opportunities for control. Cairns' (1977) comment that Canadian provincial governments can develop and expand without being based on "distinct cultures, society or nation as they are conventionally understood" can be applied equally well to the subcultural blocs in the Netherlands.

Cairns (1977) notes that powerful provincial governments have arisen in spite of the lack of strong provincial communities. It can be argued that the lack of strong provincial identities may actually enhance the power of provincial governments vis-à-vis the federal government and each other. It was suggested earlier that blocs based on non-stigmatic characteristics, such as religious blocs, tended to be authoritarian and were better able to co-ordinate the perceptions of their memberships, while blocs based on stigmata tend to be more democratic. Elites of religiously-based blocs also have more control over their followers by virtue of having control over the spiritual values of the group. Provincial elites in Canada rarely have control over the ideology or spiritual values of the province; they do have, however, a monopoly position on many services, and citizens would have to move physically to a different province in order to obtain qualitatively better services. Furthermore, those who leave frequently do so without voicing complaints (i.e., exit-without-voice), thereby reducing pressure on provincial governments. Competition from non-governing political parties does impose some constraints on the behaviour of provincial governments, but opposition criticism usually is not terribly strong. Particularly in stands concerning the relationship of the province with the federal government, there frequently is unanimity between the provincial government and opposition leaders. Provincial governments often can protect themselves by blaming the federal government. Cabinet secrecy, the tendency of the electoral system to over-compensate parties with a plurality of the vote, and party discipline, all help to concentrate power and influence in the hands of provincial leaders. (Simeon, 1972; Watts, 1970). Furthermore, it gives provincial elites considerable scope for manoeuvering when negotiating with other governments.

By contrast, the existence of a well-defined provincial society may impose distinct limits on what a provincial government can do. Survey evidence has shown that French-Canadians see the relationship between Quebec and the rest of Canada in zero-sum terms; that is, Quebec puts more into confederation than it is getting in return. Many English-Canadians feel the same way towards Quebec.[12] This puts constraints on Quebec political elites, since they are much more susceptible to competition from counter-elites for the reasons cited earlier in the section on ethnicity. Since French-Canadians are less able to relocate to other provinces, they also are less likely to vote with their feet but more likely to apply pressure on the government itself. This leaves the government less free to negotiate with the other governments. The Victoria Charter fell through in 1971 when Premier Bourassa felt he was unable to get sufficient support from his caucus and the Quebec legislative assembly.[13] Quebec governments since the early 1960's have probably been subject to more constraint by the electorate than have the other provincial governments.

In summary, institutional frameworks in combination with other factors or resources, such as territory, economic viability, the interdependence of classes within populations (which are often territorially based), can be used by local elites to increase the scope and power of their governments. Once interests become entrenched within instutitions, they become extremely difficult to dismantle. Thus, in many cases only tacit support is required for institutions to be viable.

This appears to be the case for many of the provincial governments in Canada. The fact that many provincial governments are responsive to the needs of their citizens in a variety of areas gives them a great deal of scope in dealing with other provinces as well as with the federal government. In Quebec, the provisions of the BNA Act concerning provincial control over education and related matters, played an important role in protecting and furthering French-Canadian culture, but as the period of the Province of Canada between 1840 and 1867 illustrated, French-Canadian culture was capable of surviving without any formal institutional guarantees. French-Canadian culture probably has had as much effect on the operation of institutions as *vice versa*. The distribution of powers and provincial institutions have given the predominantly English-language provinces considerable leeway for developing their own powers. In Quebec, the cultural distinctiveness of that province has, in recent times, acted to constrain elites in their exercise of power, particularly with regard to the power to negotiate with other governments. It is this imbalance in the position of Quebec on the one hand, and the English-language provinces on the other, along with economic disparities between several of the provinces, which helps to explain the inability of all eleven governments to resolve basic issues. Furthermore, the rule of proportionality which prevails in Belgium and the Netherlands is not really applicable in Canada because the resolution of many issues requires some governments winning and others losing.

G. Conclusion

Duchacek (1970) notes that in federal systems, subnational units are often subject to contradictory feelings of "let us alone" and "let us in". Subunits appear to want autonomy, but simultaneously perceive the need for some kind of association. The degree to which subunits actually express these feelings and the degree to which they are capable of maintaining autonomy and bargaining successfully on matters which affect the federation as a whole, is dependent on several factors. In this section, I have discussed how cleavage patterns are related to the development of distinct communities, the nature of inter-communal conflict, and, in turn, how this affects elite compromise.

Different cleavages vary widely in the effect they have on peoples' behaviour and in the manner in which they can be used by political elites to mobilize individuals. If religion is the basis of political community, then elites will tend to have a high degree of control over followers, in part by virtue of their control over spiritual values. In the case of linguistic or racial subcultures, elites within such communities will be in a much weaker position vis-à-vis their followers.

In modern societies class conflict is often seen in positive-sum terms by the parties involved; workers and managers often concede that both classes perform necessary functions, and they often resolve their differences by imposing increased costs upon other groups or society as a whole. Conflicts between ethnic communities, on the other hand, are much more likely to be perceived in zero-sum terms. Characteristics such as race or language are readily identifiable, which makes it easier to single out a community for discrimination. And when discrimination does occur, it is more likely to be obvious to members of the community. Conversion costs are high, so members are unlikely to switch to other communities to take advantage of resources denied to them in their community of origin. Aside from any primordial bonds which might exist, this fact alone would increase pressures for collective change.

Examples of religious communities without other cleavages are difficult to find. Evidence from the Netherlands, however, suggests that demands made of the larger society by leaders of religious communities tend to be for equal access to the resources of the state in areas which are deemed to be important in protecting core religious values. In spite of protracted struggles over issues such as parochial education, religion has had a moderating influence in countries like the Netherlands, Belgium, and Canada by dampening both economic and ethnic conflict.

Territory offers a distinctive criterion for positive or negative treatment, and also a basis for the development of perceptions of discrimination. The distribution of resources such as land, timber, oil, and other commodities, is invariably uneven in any nation. Thus, there will inevitably be imbalance between different territorial units. The impact of economic development also tends to be uneven. If central governments are actively involved in promoting the growth of industries and related enterprises, then perceptions of discrimination can easily arise on the part of regions which have missed out on economic opportunities. This means that issues involving territories can lead to demands for redistribution of some valued resource. Specialization within territorial units can lead to increasing interdependence between them if they serve as markets for one another. On the other hand, creation of a series of independent economies within a federal system might alleviate complaints of inequalities on a short-term basis, but would also mean greater inefficiency and general economic decline, which, in the long-run, would lead either to the perception that other units are no longer needed or to the exacerbation of differences as the units compete with one another for industries.

Institutions in and of themselves do not result in the creation of distinct communities. They can, however, encourage the growth of one or another type of community. In the Netherlands, the proportional electoral system and the proportional allocation of state funds in the areas of education, welfare, and broadcasting, greatly encouraged the growth of religious and secular subcultures. The BNA Act encouraged the growth of strong provincial governments in Canada. Institutions and constitutional provisions corresponded to the needs of regional interests who used these institutions to enhance greatly their power and influence. This power can be used, and has been used, to place essentially redistributive demands on the federal system. On the other hand, their influence is sufficiently broad that, if the political will is there, provincial leaders, particularly those of English-language provinces, are in a position to compromise without unduly alientating their support base.

The five sources of cleavage discussed in this section have been treated as distinct categories largely for purposes of exposition. Rarely is a community based on a single source of cleavage. Religious communities often have an ethnic component, while ethnic communities frequently have a territorial base. In looking at any community, however, it is important to look at the relationship between the members of the community and their leaders. The literature on federalism frequently takes communities as given, or tends to personify collectivities, attributing to them collective personalities. In doing so, it neglects the fact that communities can vary greatly in cohesion, particularly regarding the ability of leaders to mobilize and control members of the community.

To what extent has this contributed to an understanding of Canadian federalism? There are distinct parallels between Belgium and Canada with respect to the religious and linguistic cleavage. There are strong similarities in the effect institutions have in encouraging the growth of provincial and religious/secular communities in Canada and the Netherlands, respectively. The persistence of state divisions and institutions in the relatively homogeneous society of Australia points to the possibility that similar forces are at work in Canada, which may account for the longevity of Canadian provincial institutions. All these examples, however, concern particular aspects of the Canadian state. Unfortunately, when all the elements are put together, it appears that there really is no example quite like the Canadian case. In the Netherlands, all the blocs are based primarily on organization. In Belgium, the division is between two linguistic communities which are approximately equal in size. Australia has a federal system which lacks an ethnic cleavage and in which there are fewer discrepancies between the states in terms of economic development. Canada is quite different from these nations.

What is important about divided countries, and federal countries in particular, is the character of the relations which exist between the constitutent units. We are able to make generalizations about systems where the units are based either primarily on organization or primarily on ethnicity. In Canada, we have a number of vertical segments (to use Lijphart's terminology) based primarily on organization, co-existing with a single segment based primarily on language and culture. This arrangement really has no parallel. The possibility of choosing models for Canada to follow is severely restricted, at least in terms of predicting what the consequences might be if a whole new set of institutions were introduced.

Another feature distinguishes Canada from the other examples, one which complicates further the problem of comparative analysis, but which also may contain a lesson for Canada. In Canada there are no firm rules, formal or informal, which order the relations between the different levels of government, particularly with regard to major questions. One can argue that Canada's constitution is so flexible as to be almost non-existent in a number of key areas. No firm rules have evolved to take the place of constitutional provisions which have been rendered irrelevant over the years.[14] One inference which can be drawn is that societies like Canada can survive only if firm rules are lacking, and this may have been true for the past one hundred years. However, given the changes in the forces buffeting the Canadian federal system, this might not be a safe assumption to make for the next one hundred years. Other divided countries do have firm rules, sometimes arrived at in a Grand Compromise arising from a crisis similar to those now facing Canada — and there appears to be some benefit in having such crises. If there is one thing we can say about societies like Switzerland and the United States, it is that they have clear rules for revising arrangements between the constitutent units and for the creation of additional units.

Unfortunately, in nations like Switzerland and the United States, constitutional arrangements often were imposed on a minority of units by a majority through the use of force. Perhaps one reason why this has not occured in Canada is because Canadians and Canadian politicians have been civilized when it comes to settling political differences. As problems become more intractable, however, the civility of Canadian political leaders may not be an adequate basis for maintaining a viable federal system. It is hoped that what will evolve out of the current Canadian crisis is a firm set of rules, a Grand Compromise perhaps, which will be perceived as being legitimate by the constituent units and the citizenry as a whole. What is currently at stake is not so much the distribution and redistribution of valued goods and services (where there has been agreement in the past: e.g., equalization, Canada Pension Plan, etc.) but rather, the procedural rules through which accommodation can occur. These rules are currently lacking; as one commentator noted in 1971, "In the long run, this is too fragile a basis to work on. In times of stress, democracies can survive by applying intelligent legal rules and sticking to them." (Van der Esch, 1971).

Comparative analysis, however, can also help us in defining the substance of these rules. Furthermore, on the basis of our analysis, we might want to offer suggestions, too, as to the kind of communities whose growth should be promoted or discouraged. Recently, a number of proposals for constitutional change have argued for a decision-making process primarily involving governmental elites representing territorial and/or ethnic communities. The following chapter evaluates these so-called "consociational" solutions to the problem of Canadian political integration and puts forward some alternative solutions, whose viability is based on the encouragement of broad-based non-territorial and non-ethnic communities.

Footnotes

1. In fact, Wheare did devote considerable time to the way federal systems actually worked. His well-known definition concerning the co-ordinate and independent status of the different levels of government can be seen best as a yardstick for assessing the degree to which federal societies approach being a true federal polity.

2. Most of the literature on cleavages is concerned with the reinforcement, cross-cutting, and intensity of cleavages. Religious, class, and ethnic cleavages are often assumed to be similar. Little effort is made to distinguish between cleavages in terms of their impact. Lipset and Rokkan (1967), for example, see the generation of party systems in Western Europe mainly as a function of coalitions and confrontations between elites who have bases of support in the wider society. They give little indication, however, as to how elites (e.g., the Church, landowners) can mobilize support in some countries but not in others, or about the extent to which elites are constrained by their followers in developing coalitions.

3. Why confessional organizations were successful in some countries depended on the role of the Church and the arrival of industrialization. In countries like Germany, the church authorities took Pope Leo XIII's encyclical *Rerum Novarum* quite seriously. This was not the case in either France or Italy. Secondly, the industrial revolution came to Germany and the Netherlands much later. This allowed religious leaders to profit from the experiences of France and England, where the industrial revolution had come much earlier. See Fogarty (1957).

4. Quoted in Leih (1962), p. 135. The leader referred to is Abraham Kuiper, who was leader of the Calvinist Anti-Revolutionary Party in the Netherlands.

5. The provision of social welfare services has always been very important for the church (see the Tremblay Report, Kwavnick, 1973). The decline in manpower in the late 1950's and early 1960's made the performance of these tasks much more difficult, and as a result, control in this area ebbed away to public institutions (Guindon, 1964).

6. See the report on this in the *Star-Phoenix*, Saskatoon, March 18, 1978.

7. Rabushka and Shepsle (1972), in their well-known work on democratic instability, argue that political competition in ethnically-divided societies is likely to be intense and characterized by the devaluation of compromise positions. This leads to the propensity of leaders within ethnic blocs to outbid each other. The reasoning is essentially circular, however: Rabushka and Shepsle state that multi-ethnic societies have a lot of conflict because such societies have a lot of conflict. In terms of their argument, there is no reason why leaders will always take more extreme positions. I have argued that leaders of a community based on stigmatic characteristics will find it easier to take more extreme positions. If a community is based primarily on organization (e.g., religion, province), this makes it difficult to exclude outsiders from public goods intended for distribution primarily to that group. Criteria such as race or language make it much easier to exclude outsiders. The same holds true for costs. Rabushka and Shepsle imply that there are no limits to extremism. I would argue that there are limits. Middle-class elements in an ethnic community may see positive elements in redistributive policies favouring their community. However, they may also recognize that at a certain point massive redistribution may harm the economy of the nation to a degree whereby their own position would also be affected. For example, in Quebec there is general support for language policies restricting the use of English. Such policies would have the result of redistributing valued positions to French-Canadians,and even French-Canadians already occupying important positions would not be averse to policies of this kind for reasons having to do with a sense of kinship, opportunities for their offspring, and so on. Demands for total separation of Quebec from the rest of Canada meet with a less favourable response in large part because such a drastic move might cause irrevocable harm to the economy of Quebec, harming the well-being not only of the middle-classes but of other classes as well.

8. Simeon and Elkins (1980) note that from 1965 to 1974 Canadians generally have come to see provincial governments as more important than the federal government.

9. In the early years of Canadian Confederation, it was often possible for the federal government to make side payments to the provinces, and for federal politicians to promise one thing in one area of the country and something quite different in other areas. See Dawson and Ward (1970), pp. 99-118. With the improvement in communications this is no longer possible.

10. See also H. Flanz (1968) for a detailed discussion of the West Indies case.

11. Sproule-Jones (1975) denies that his framework involves competition between different levels of government. At the same time, his scheme requires overlapping jurisdictions, so that consumers can choose which level of government is best able to provide the appropriate service. To assume that governments under these circumstances will not compete with one another is naive.

12. Below is some data on the perceived inequality in the distribution of the benefits from the existing institutional arrangements:

	Total	Quebec
Benefits are divided		
evenly	33%	23%
unevenly	46%	54%
Don't know/No answer	21%	23%
	100%	100%

Who Benefits Most*		
Quebec	32%	6%
Other	68%	94%
	100%	100%

Who Benefits Least*		
Quebec	13%	40%
Other	87%	60%
	100%	100%

* Asked only of those saying benefits are divided unevenly, excludes non-respondents.

Source: *CROP Survey*, March, 1977.

13. Note that in Quebec since 1960, three different parties have formed governments. Simeon notes that in the case of the Victoria Charter in 1971, Quebec was the only province where there was wide-spread interest in, and opposition to, the provisions of the Charter.

14. In Canada, although the governments themselves are highly institutionalized, the rules governing relations between the governments are not. There is no permanent staff associated with the major arena for resolving differences, the federal-provincial conference. Some analysts, like Simeon, have identified certain informal rules and strategies used by most actors during bargaining strategies, but these do not constitute rules for allocating resources. What informal rules do exist seem to change from decade to decade. Note the shift from the co-operative federalism phase prevailing during the period 1945 to the early 1960's, to the more combatitive form of executive federalism prevailing currently.

3 Canada and the Consociational Model

In grappling with the problem of Canadian unity, one major question arises: what strategies can be employed to mitigate or override the centrifugal tendencies in the Canadian federation? Here, I will examine some of the literature on political integration and evaluate in detail one specific model of political integration – the consociational politics model. The model stresses the importance of elite accommodation and the insulation and non-participation of citizens. It has been used by Canadian social scientists for both analytical and prescriptive purposes. How accurate is it as a description of political reality in Canada and in other countries? Should we encourage the growth of mechanisms and institutions to promote consociationalism in Canada? Or could such a strategy backfire and create more problems than might be solved? In part, the task will be to identify institutions, both actual and proposed, which may help promote consociationalism, although they are not usually considered consociational.[1] I will also argue that the model developed by William Riker (1964), concerning the importance of the party system, is probably superior both for explaining the Canadian case and developing strategies to promote political integration.

A. Political Integration and Consociationalism

What do we mean by political integration? It involves the forces holding a political community together, as well as the factors which initiated the formation of a nation. One theme in the literature states that there should be a parallel growth in central institutions for collective decision-making and in mass orientations which legitimate them. This is the approach taken by Karl Deutsch *et al* in a work on Western Europe written in 1957. Deutsch developed a model of political integration which specified nine basic and necessary conditions. He was mainly interested in the possible

62

integration of the Western European countries into one nation-state. Among the nine conditions which Deutsch felt had to be present for political integration to take place were, for example, "a distinctive way of life", "expectation of economic gains", and "unbroken links of social communication" (p. 58). Deutsch *et al* have been widely criticized, for example by Birch, 1966. It is suggested that the conditions they specified are neither necessary nor sufficient: in fact, there are cases where the nine conditions prevailed but no integration resulted. Alternatively, there are examples of political integration where many of the nine conditions did not exist.

Deutsch *et al* were writing within the framework of international relations, but the field of political integration is also of great interest to students of federalism. For example, K.C. Wheare (1947) listed six conditions necessary for the creation of a federation, among them military and economic insecurity on the part of contiguous states and similarity of political institutions. The same criticisms of Deutsch *et al* can also be made of Wheare. Furthermore, both Deutsch and Wheare, in specifying their required conditions, are concerned mainly with the formation of political communities, and not with the forces important to sustaining them.

William Riker (1964), another writer on federalism, is also concerned with the conditions leading to the federal bargain, and with the forces and mechanisms which sustain a federal system over time. Riker stresses that political parties are the critical forces linking the constituent units in a federal society, but he neglects other important factors. In particular, he downplays the possibility that the role of parties could be played by intergovernmental bureaucratic or executive institutions. For example, in Canada the federal-provincial conferences are important arenas where many federal-provincial differences are resolved. Indeed, Simeon (1977) suggests that the federal-provincial conference has largely replaced parties in the integration of regional and provincial forces in Canada.

The literature of political integration will not be explored in detail, but one particular model of political integration, recently in vogue, will be discussed. This model is usually referred to as the consociational democracy model. It is directly concerned with the political viability and continuation of deeply-divided societies, and stresses the importance of political factors. The model emphasizes the importance of elite accommodation, and suggests that deep cleavages within a society can be overcome if political elites co-operate with one another. One Canadian political scientist, S.J. Noel (1974, 1977a, 1977b), has used the consociational model to explain the past maintenance of the Canadian federal system. He has also argued that if the Canadian federation is to continue, Canadian politicians should adopt further consociational practices.

Noel is not the only political scientist to have applied the consociational model to the Canadian situation. A standard undergraduate text on Canadian politics by Van Loon and Whittington (1976) makes explicit use of the consociational model for analytical purposes, as does Robert Presthus (1974) in his *Political Leaders, Bureaucrats and Pressure Groups: Elite Accommodation in Canadian Politics*. Richard Simeon (1972), in his book *Federal Provincial Diplomacy* also draws on the consociational politics literature, but suggests the conditions for its successful operation probably no longer exist in Canada. Kenneth McRae's (1974a) edited collection of readings on the subject, *Consociational Democracy*, contains a number of articles analysing Canadian history and politics from the consociational perspective. Most closely associated with the consociational model is Arend Lijphart, who examined several societies, including Canada, and in 1977 concluded that:

> The future of the Canadian political system will depend to a large extent on whether it moves in the direction of greater consociationalism and, as a result, greater stability and unity, or in the direction of a more centrifugal regime with a partition of the country as its most likely outcome. (1977a, p. 129)

Thus, the consociational democracy theme is applied to the Canadian context not only to analyse Canadian politics, but also to prescribe a means for resolving the problems confronting the Canadian Federation.

When and where did the consociational model originate? In its modern form, it was developed by the Dutch political scientist Arend Lijphart (1968), as he tried to account for the stability of the Netherlands which was on the surface, until the mid-1960's, deeply divided by social and religious cleavages. Other variants of the consociational model, which employ somewhat different terminology, were developed by J. Steiner (1974) and Val Lorwin (1974) to explain the functioning of countries like Switzerland, Belgium, and Austria. Despite their differences in terminology, all these writers focus on the behaviour of elites to explain political stability in deeply-divided societies.

According to Lijphart, consociational democracy is a result of deliberate efforts by leaders of rival subcultures to counteract the immobilizing and destabilizing effects of cultural fragmentation (linguistic, ethnic, and the like). It is government by elite cartel which is designed to turn a democracy with a fragmented political culture into a stable one. Implicit in the model is the idea that certain societies have such pronounced cleavages that only deliberate joint effort by elites can produce a stable political system. If elites do not act together, then civil war can result: in the case of a federal system, the component units can disagree and secede. While writers like Deutsch stress patterns of communication and the development of a common consensus, Lijphart instead focuses largely on elites: a common consensus among people within a divided society is not essential to a democracy's survival.

The attractiveness of the consociational model to Canadians concerned with national unity should be obvious: mutual feelings of accommodation among the Canadian people is not the issue. A federal disaster can be averted by the elites through their own behaviour and actions. Thus, the adoption of consociational practices implies accommodative behaviour on the part of elites to overcome dissension at the mass level.[2]

There are problems with Lijphart's model, however. There is evidence that the model may not even adequately account for the Dutch case, and this, in turn, has implications for applying the model to Canada. There is considerable question whether the kind of system described by Lijphart exists − or has ever existed − in the Netherlands, despite its being his quintessential consociational democracy. The factors which account for the stability of the Dutch system are rather different from those Lijphart identifies. Indeed, there is something we can call consociational democracy in the Netherlands and the behaviour of the elites is important, but this differs a fair bit from Lijphart's model. Accommodation in Dutch society is not restricted to the elites: they are probably just as active in fostering cleavages and political conflict as they are in bridging them.

No model should be applied uncritically to the Canadian situation. Steven Wolinetz (1978), indeed, said that the consociational model is not applicable to Canada, but this is not the position taken here. There *are* distinct parallels between Canada and the Netherlands. In defining these parallels, much can be learned about the Canadian political system. The conclusions, however, do *not* necessarily imply adopting strategies which promote consociationalism: in fact, they suggest the opposite.

B. Consociationalism in the Netherlands

How does a consociational society work? A brief look at the Netherlands provides an answer. In that country of 14 million people, there are five blocs or subcultures: Catholic, Protestant, Calvinist, socialist, and liberal. How distinctive the blocs are is still debated: some people put the two protestant blocs together, while others group the socialist and liberal blocs as a single secular bloc, thereby reducing the number to three (Daalder, 1974b; Lijphart, Kruijt, 1974). According to Lijphart (1968), each bloc is culturally distinctive, with goals and interests at variance with the other blocs.[3] How is conflict between them regulated? Lijphart lists four basic conditions for the success of a consociational democracy. First, the elites must be able to accommodate the divergent interests and demands of the subcultures. They must be able to transcend cleavages by common effort with the elites of rival subcultures. Next, they must be strongly committed to the maintenance of the system. Finally, they must be aware of the perils of political fragmentation (Lijphart, 1974, p. 79). Basically, Lijphart assumes that the cleavages dividing these blocs are deep and mutually reinforcing but that conflict between the blocs can be averted and that a stable system of governing can arise through elite co-operation. Potential antagonism at the mass level is minimized through co-operation at the elite level. Other factors Lijphart identifies as important in the consociational system include elite agreement on certain rules of the game, and a minimum level of popular national feeling. These factors are rather *ad hoc*, however, since Lijphart added them later to his original model.

Certain serious empirical and theoretical problems are inherent in the model.[4] The notion of elite co-operation is one problem, and Daalder (1974a) points out that in the Netherlands co-operation between elites has been a tradition since medieval times, predating significantly the basic cleavages Lijphart identifies. The divisions between religious and secular blocs did not develop until the turn of the century. Thus, elite co-operation in Dutch society did not arise from the crisis of political conflict; it predated the crisis.

There are further problems related to the distinctiveness of the different blocs or subcultures. How deep, in fact, are the cleavages dividing the subcultures? What is the nature of conflict between the blocs? To what degree is co-operation between the different blocs lacking at the mass level? If it can be shown that the differences between the blocs (in terms of ideology, culture, or substantive issues) are not great in the Netherlands, this would weaken the model's successful export to countries where cleavages are deeper or more intense. Furthermore, if it can be shown that co-operation between blocs in the Netherlands exists not only at the elite level but also at the mass level, this casts further doubt on the causal status of elite behaviour.

If we look at institutions and behaviour, the different blocs in the Netherlands do indeed appear to be rigidly divided. Each major bloc has its own political party, television and radio broadcasting facilities, and newspapers, and most have their own educational facilities (from kindergarten through university), health care systems, and so on. The organizational networks of the different blocs were wide-ranging, too. For example, as a Catholic, you could join a Catholic tennis club or Catholic birdwatching society, and associate almost exclusively with other Catholics: this was true, at least, until the mid-1960's. In fact, people generally spent their leisure time within the parameters of their respective blocs. In the important area of communication, Catholics subscribe to Catholic newspapers, and allegedly only listen to Catholic radio programs and only watch Catholic television. Similarly, the vast majority of Calvinists follow the same pattern.

There are certain areas, however, where these differences are less apparent. Although there is a distinctive literature which is written for and by Catholics, and another for and by Protestants, there is also a broad secular literature. In terms of the books people actually read, socio-religious cleavages tend to disappear. Even during the 1950's, the heyday of consociationalism, the vast majority of Catholics read secular or non-religious novels, and the same was true of Protestants. Presently television and radio audiences pay little attention to whether the program is Catholic, socialist or Protestant, although, by bloc, they are formally affiliated with one of the broadcasting organizations (Gadourek, 1956; Bakvis, forthcoming, 1981).

Neither is there much cultural distinctiveness. Catholics, Protestants, and socialists tend to enjoy the same kind of activities and to have similar interests, and the organizations of the different blocs offer their members remarkably similar services. For example, member trade unions of the Catholic trade union federation offer programs and services very similar to those offered by the socialist trade unions (Windmuller, 1969).[5] During collective bargaining, the trade unions of the different blocs — socialist, Catholic, and Protestant — will invariably adopt common policies and bargain jointly. Furthermore, there is often no conflict *per se* between the blocs. There is, instead, general agreement that people in the different blocs will, according to their socio-religious persuasion, spend much of their leisure time within their own bloc, and will join its trade union and other similar organizations.

Cleavages in the Netherlands are supposed to be mutually reinforcing. According to Lijphart, this is so because there is no overlapping membership. For example, a Catholic is usually not a member of a socialist trade union. However, within the Catholic bloc, there are Catholic workers, shopkeepers, and factory owners who have distinct interests and who think of themselves as working-class, middle-class, and so on. Thus, membership in organizations is reinforcing only in the sense that all the organizations to which people belong tend to carry the same label, whether Catholic, Protestant, socialist, or liberal. The liberal and socialist blocs tend to have distinct economic interests which are at variance with one another, whereas the Catholic and Protestant blocs on an aggregate level have similar economic interests. Within the Catholic bloc, a large portion of Catholics are working-class. As a result, particularly before the changes in the Dutch party system in the mid-1960's[6], positions taken by Catholic leaders on economic issues were often quite close to those taken by socialist leaders. This in itself facilitates co-operation between the political elites.

Co-operation within the Dutch consociational system takes place not only between political elites but also between economic elites, as is the case when leaders of the different trade unions and federations co-operate on a given issue. Considerable co-operation is also evident between the different bloc leaders in organizations like welfare groups. The Social Economic Council, a major Cabinet advisory body, has a membership drawn from the major economic organizations in Dutch society — trade unions and employer organizations from each of the major blocs, as well as members from the government (Lijphart, 1968). Within the Social Economic Council, leaders of the confessional and socialist trade unions tend to take common positions which are often opposed to those of the confessional and liberal employer federations (Windmuller, 1969). Thus, at the elite level and in a variety of political and non-political sectors, there is considerable co-operation; conflict, when it occurs, frequently cuts across religious lines. It is misleading, therefore, to assume that all interaction between blocs occurs only among political leaders.

Co-operation occurs at all levels of political life. Eighty percent of the 900 municipal district councils in the Netherlands include representatives of the different blocs on a proportional basis (the remaining 20% of districts are homogeneously Catholic or Protestant), yet here too, co-operation and consensus are the rule. Even in non-political sectors, at the lower levels we find examples of accommodation. The Hungarian sociologist, Ivan Gadourek (1956), describes how Dutch factory workers belonging to the three different trade union locals — Catholic, Protestant and socialist — periodically gathered to discuss issues of common concern. Their opinions and proposed solutions were then forwarded within the three trade union federations to the provincial level, and, if necessary, to the national level.

At all levels of organizational activity it is necessary to have a certain amount of co-operation. In a small community, for example, Catholic and Protestant health care organizations might share a building. Interest groups with common economic concerns but different "spiritual" backgrounds will often make joint demands to the government. As long as proportionality is maintained, and as long as the groups agree not to raid one another's membership, co-operation is possible at all levels and within all sectors. There is no evidence that there is more co-operation at the elite level than at the mass level.

In fact, it is possible to argue that there is less co-operation at the elite level. Hans Daalder (1966) noted the lengthy duration of negotiations leading to the formation of coalition cabinets in the Netherlands. Among the actions of elites hindering cabinet formation are ones involving personal interests, career advancement, and retaliation against other individuals either in the same or another party (Daalder, 1966, p. 222). Achieving agreement on bloc representation is, of course, a major difficulty in cabinet formation. It would be misleading, though, to believe that Dutch political elites always want to bridge their differences for the well-being of the nation, or that there is considerable animosity at the mass level between, for example, Catholics and Protestants.

So why do these blocs exist if people belonging to the different blocs have similar interests, and if co-operation is not just restricted to elites? Why don't people simply realign themselves according to their basic social and economic interests? Ironically, leadership is the crucial reason. In the Netherlands, elites — rather than bridging cleavages — have been largely responsible for creating and politicizing them. During the latter part of the nineteenth century, elites used religious issues to create vast organizational networks based on socio-religious differences. This required considerable political and organizational entrepreneurship. Catholic and Protestant leaders were the main entrepreneurs, and their main objective was control over education.

In 1917, the educational issue was resolved by giving Catholics and Protestants full state support for their parochial schools. The Catholics and the Orthodox Calvinists had long fought for equal status for their parochial schools alongside the state secular schools (Daalder, 1966). At the same time, the 1917 "Pacification" agreement provided for the extension of the franchise and for a proportional electoral system, things the Social Democratic Party had promoted for some time. While it established the principle of proportionality with regard to education and electoral representation, in later years the Pacification became a template for organizing other areas of policy. With the arrival of radio broadcasting in the 1920's, for example, leaders of the different blocs demanded that broadcasting facilities and time be shared proportionally. The same was true for health and welfare: subsidies for hospitals, recreational activities, and health insurance were allocated by the State to the different socio-economic-religious blocs on a proportional basis.

Organizational entrepreneurship is very important, as can be seen by looking at turn-of-the-century Catholic Church and lay organizations in the Netherlands. Catholic priests and Catholic trade union leaders began organizing workers, often well before the socialists. The aim, of course, was to ensure that Catholic workers remained within the confines of the Catholic Church and subculture. This was achieved by making sure that workers in Catholic trade unions received services and protection equivalent to what the socialist trade unions offered.[7] Once the various organizations were established, it was important to continue providing decent services to maintain a loyal clientele. This was the case with the socialist, Catholic, and Protestant organizations, and, to a much lesser extent, with the liberal organizations. Catholics joined Catholic trade unions not only because they were Catholic, but also because the differences between Catholic and socialist trade union benefits and policies were not substantial. If the services of a particular organization seriously deteriorated, or if the branch of that organization was absent, people often would join an alternative organization locally with a different bloc affiliation, resulting in a complete change in bloc identification. The Catholic Church recognized this early in the twentieth century. In Rotterdam between 1910 and 1920, the socialist trade unions were much better organized than the Catholic ones. As a result, many Catholics joined socialist trade unions and subsequently left the Catholic Church (Rogier, 1953). The flow of Catholics and some Protestants switching to the secular blocs was mainly one way, with the pattern seldom reversed. After the first World War, however, this flow reduced to a trickle until the 1960's, when, in the case of several Catholics influenced by deconfessionalization, the trickle became a flood. (See Bakvis, 1978; Wolinetz, 1973).

Thus, there was, and still is, competition between the blocs. The vast range of organizational networks existed to fulfill the needs of and provide services for their clients, and they all had to meet the competition. On the whole, the socialists, the Protestants and particularly the Catholics were quite successful in this. The quality of Catholic newspapers, for example, was relatively high, and the same was true of Catholic broadcasting (Bakvis, 1978, p. 50). In fact, if one examines the kind of programmes broadcast on Catholic television during the 1950's, they were mainly situation comedies, popular movies, variety shows, quiz shows, and the like. In the Protestant and Catholic blocs, the religious element in television programming was, and still is, present, but is only one of several elements.

Frequently, strong pressures were applied by the local protestant pastor or parish priest to ensure clientele loyalty to their organizations, and sanctions were often severe. Economic benefits were important, in the sense that services offered by confessional organizations were just as good — if not better — than those offered by the secular blocs. A Catholic contemplating switching to another organization or bloc would not gain much. The services or benefits he might receive from another bloc, (socialist if he was a worker, or liberal if he was middle- or upper-class), probably would not differ significantly from those offered by Catholic organizations. Sanctions by the Church, pressures from family and friends, and other social and psychological elements were strong deterrents to renouncing Catholicism. For a Catholic to remain loyal to Catholic organizations was essentially a matter of common sense, and there was little reason for an individual to leave the confines of his bloc. This loyalty did not necessarily involve hostility, and there was general agreement that people belonging to different blocs might co-operate in certain areas other than social or religious.

Further reasons for the cohesion of the different blocs involved the ability of elites to define who was, and who was not, a member of a particular bloc. The Catholic bloc was considered by far the most cohesive. (See Laponce, 1960, p. 139). This was due largely to the more powerful religious sanctions the Catholic Church had available, such as excommunication. Within a bloc such as the liberals, which was a subculture largely by default, there was much more dissension because the leadership did not have as powerful sanctions to ensure cohesion.

An additional factor which worked to the advantage of bloc leaders was the relative homogeneity of Dutch society with regard to colour, ethnicity, and language. Discrimination, where it did exist (and there was a fair amount against Catholics), was not always obvious because generally people looked and dressed similarly. Thus, members of the different blocs were often dependent upon instructions from leaders about a given situation. This gave the leaders an advantage by providing them with scope for manoeuvring. They could increase or decrease tensions, depending upon the circumstances.

This sketch of Dutch society and politics differs from Lijphart's description. The major feature of Dutch society is that cleavages are based primarily on ideology and organization. Ideology rationalizes and legitimizes the differences between the blocs, but these differences exist largely because of the organizational talents of the leaders of the different religious or ideological groupings. Important, too, is that the rule of allocation is primarily proportional: goods in society are distributed among the different blocs on a proportional basis. Catholics, for example, are *not* given more money per capita than Protestants or liberals, and this has always been the case. This rule of proportionality is of major importance in ensuring the stability of the system. Issues involving redistribution of scarce resources between classes or regions are often fought over and worked out within the confines of the different blocs, or in bodies like the Social Economic Council, where they cut across religious differences. Thus, really important redistributional issues do not provide fuel to fan any flames of bitterness arising from the ideological differences between blocs.

C. Consociationalism in Canada: Part I

How can the consociational model be applied to the Canadian situation? Defining the lines of cleavage and the subcultures is a real problem. S.J. Noel has gone furthest in attempting to apply the consociational model to Canada (1974). In doing so, he has made certain adjustments to make the model fit. "The term subculture could be interpreted in a number of ways. It could be taken, for example, to refer to English-Canada and

French-Canada, or to a number of distinct regions, such as the Maritimes, Quebec, Ontario and the West — but most usefully perhaps as 'provinces' " (p. 265). There are good reasons for interpreting Lijphart's model in terms of provinces. In the Canadian federal system, the provinces provide a tangible institutional framework for articulating and aggregating local and regional interests, which are then accommodated at the federal level (McRae, 1974b, p. 239). This accommodation occurs through the various mechanisms of federal-provincial interaction. Thus, according to Noel (1977b), elite accommodation takes place at several levels: in the patterns of communication and consultation among senior provincial civil servants; in meetings of such interprovincial bodies as the Council of Ministers of Education; in federal-provincial conferences; and in numerous federal boards and commissions with provincial representation (p. 156). According to Noel, one of the major institutions is the federal cabinet (1974, 1977b).

Noel's definition of subcultures has been criticized by Kenneth McRae (1974b), who argues that provinces cannot be seen as distinct subcultures. If the analogy is to become complete, McRae argues, the component units of the federation must coincide sufficiently with distinct subcultural coundaries. In India, for example, state boundaries have been drawn to coincide closely with linguistic and cultural boundaries. Certain of the Swiss cantons provide a further example. In Canada, McRae warns, one should not assume an automatic coincidence of provincial and subcultural boundaries. He says that it is difficult to see the ten provinces, or even the five regions, of Canada as distinctive spiritual (or ideological) blocs analogous to the ones in European countries like the Netherlands. Thus, McRae (1974) states that if we compare Nova Scotia with Ontario or B.C. in terms of value systems, life styles, and general cultural patterns, it is likely that we would find greater differences within provinces than between them, and that inter-regional variations within Canada would be, by most criteria, significantly fewer than within many countries of Europe (pp. 239-240).

Here, however, McRae is wrong. To begin with, it has been shown that within the Netherlands the different blocs are not very distinctive in terms of life style, values, and so on. Furthermore, the differences between classes within the blocs in the Netherlands are probably greater than the differences between the blocs. In fact, there is some evidence for this in Lijphart's own work (1968). As well, the blocs in the Netherlands are largely institutional, and are not at all similar to ethnic and linguistic blocs in other countries. In Belgium, the institutions associated with consociational practices and the spiritual blocs actually cut across linguistic boundaries (Lorwin, 1974). The Catholic, socialist, and liberal parties draw support from both language groups. Language differences in Belgium are reconciled *within* the spiritual blocs, and not directly in the political arena, although this has changed considerably since the early 1960's (Zolberg, 1977).

It can be argued that the Canadian provinces, except Quebec, owe their existence to institutions and political entrepreneurship (Cairns, 1977). Furthermore, differences between the provinces are much greater than is usually acknowledged. Donald Blake (1972) has examined the effect of regionalism on voting behaviour in Canada, and has noted that regionalism does have considerable impact. Richard Simeon and David Elkins (1974), in their article on regional political cultures, note that there is considerable variation not only between regions, but also between provinces within regions, in terms of basic citizen orientation towards politics. Furthermore, they note that these variations in citizen orientation, or political culture, are greater between provinces than within provinces. This suggests a high degree of similarity between the provinces in Canada and the socio-religious blocs in the Netherlands.

Wolinetz (1978), in criticizing Noel, claims that provincial governments and their officials cannot be seen as the equivalent of subcultural elites. "Provincial governments, because they can readily be removed from office, cannot speak for their constituents in the same way that subculture elites in consociational systems are said to be able to speak and bargain for their followers." Although in theory provincial governments can be readily removed from office, many provincial governments seem to display remarkable longevity. Witness Social Credit in Alberta for 35 years; Social Credit in British Columbia for 20 years; CCF/NDP in Saskatchewan for 20 years; Union Nationale in Quebec for 19 years; and the Conservatives in Ontario for more than 35 years. In instances of federal-provincial conflict, an equally important characteristic is political unanimity: the opposition parties within provinces will often support the party in government to oppose federal dominance. Recently, this was clearly the case in Saskatchewan, when the Conservative party supported the NDP in their stance on the Cigol issue.[8] Thus, a very good case can be made that provincial governments are in fact much like the subcultural elites in consociational systems.

Assuming for the moment that it is legitimate to treat provinces as subcultures, we can ask, in what way do the institutions listed by Noel operate in a consociational manner? Taking the federal Cabinet, for example, one can point to its representative character, and particularly to the emphasis placed on regional representation. Noel (1977b) notes that since constitutional convention ensures that the proceedings of Cabinet are secret, it is possible to make only indirect inferences about provincial or regional influences on decision-making. The same is true of Dutch Cabinets, however. According to Noel,

"If, ... the Cabinet is viewed in the broad framework of consociational theory, it can be seen as a mechanism of elite accommodation quite apart from the specific decisions it makes. Its importance, in other words, can be seen to lie more in its function of bringing together political leaders from the provinces and maintaining their continuous involvement in the decision-making process, than in the actual output of that process. One of the most important roles of the Prime Minister is to maintain among cabinet members drawn from the various provinces a degree of commitment to the national political system which does not exist to nearly the same extent at the popular or mass level within the provinces themselves." (p. 157)

As proof, Noel notes a number of consociational failures in Canada. For example, he points to the inability of the Diefenbaker government to involve a Quebec political elite in the process of accommodation at the federal level. This, according to Noel, was one of the major factors leading to the downfall of the Diefenbaker government. "The policies and decisions of the Diefenbaker Cabinet were not necessarily anti-Quebec; its failure to appreciate the importance of elite accommodation was." (Noel, 1977b, p. 157). The same thing was true in the case of Laurier. At the time, according to Noel, the failure of the Liberal Party in Ontario was not so much a failure of policy, as a failure to maintain the involvement at the federal level of an Ontario political elite.

I would question, however, whether the Canadian Cabinet can really be seen in consociational terms. The problem is that regional representatives in Cabinet are not appointed by the provincial governments, but by the leader of the federal party in power. Their constituency, or subculture if you like, is unclear. Although Cabinet ministers may be in charge of local federal government patronage, they are not responsible for representing specific provincial government concerns, nor do they lead specifically regional or provincial political parties. Regional representation and accommodation in federal cabinets probably can be described better in terms of brokerage theory than by the consociational model. In any case, given the weakness of the Canadian party system, representation from certain regions has recently been minimal, for example, the West under the Liberals, or Quebec under the Conservatives. If the federal cabinet is to become an important arena for elite accommodation in the future, it should be remembered that this would entail a weakening of the provincial governments, since federal Cabinet ministers would have to be given more authority over matters concerning their provinces or regions.

ERRATA

Footnote #2, Chapter 1 should appear on p. 4, line 19.

p. 2, line 4: <u>elevate</u> should read <u>evaluate</u>.

p. 8, line 11 and elsewhere: <u>MacPherson</u> should read <u>Macpherson</u>.

p. 30, line 5: <u>Haggart</u> should read <u>Hoggart</u>.

p. 65, line 18-20: Should read "Accommodation in Dutch society is not restricted to the elites. Furthermore, elites are probably just as active in fostering cleavages and political conflict as they are in bridging them."

<u>Bibliography</u>: Add: Spahn, P. B. (1978) "The Pattern of State and Local Taxation in the Federal Republic of Germany," in R. L. Mathews (ed.) State and Local Taxation. Canberra: Australian National University Press.

What about the Federal-Provincial Conference? Noel implies that this appears to be the main arena for elite accommodation in Canada. According to Noel (1977b), the existence of these conferences is more important than any agreement they produce, presumably for the same reasons as regional representation in the Cabinet. By this, he seems to suggest that these arenas and regional representation are largely symbolic. But the substantive issues discussed and the actual agreements reached are at least of equal importance. Presumably, the function of these arenas is in part to produce agreement among political leaders on specific issues. Agreement on the Canada Pension Plan, various shared cost programs, and equalization are evidence of this. Furthermore, even if one does see provincial representation in passive terms, it is still important, albeit in a negative way. One of the important features of consociational arrangements in the Netherlands and in Switzerland is the ability of a single bloc to veto any proposal which might endanger the welfare of that bloc (Rogowski, 1974).It may not be used very often, but it is nevertheless a very real (as opposed to symbolic) power, which substantially affirms the legitimacy of the arrangement. Similarly, provincial premiers can block many policies they feel might not be beneficial for their province. Many would argue, of course, that provincial premiers use this veto power too frequently, particularly in the area of constitutional reform.

Noel (1974) has noted the difficulties which arise when elite accommodation takes place within two separate arenas (cabinet and federal-provincial conferences) and between two sets of elites (federal Cabinet ministers and provincial premiers). Consociationalism combined with federalism raises the possibility of a conflict between competing federal and provincial elites within the same provincial subculture. Thus, according to Noel, the duality of political elites in a federal system makes the outcome of subcultural conflict more uncertain than it would be in a unitary state. It can be argued that in recent years, with the decline of the party system in representing all provincial interests (Smiley, 1976), the federal-provincial conference has more or less displaced the federal Cabinet as the arena for elite accommodation. In the case of certain provinces, for example Quebec, the provincial premiers appear to be the sole representatives of provincial interests. With this decline in dualism, the Canadian federation, therefore, comes much closer to approximating the consociational model. It also comes much closer to approximating one variant of what Cairns has termed the intra-state model of federalism, that is, direct provincial representation in major federal institutions.[9] This would mean affirming the identity of provinces and their governments as major actors, and generally strengthening them, at the expense of federal institutions, which might still be directly responsible to individual citizens. Proposals such as the House of the Provinces, where all representatives are appointed by the ten provincial governments, would reinforce the role of the provinces as the major actors in the process of elite accommodation.

The notion of elite accommodation, or at least the importance of it, has been questioned by a number of writers. Steven Wolinetz (1978) notes that accommodation among political leaders is a characteristic of all democratic societies: if one sees elite accommodation as very important in the consociational model, it is equally so in non-consociational systems. He claims that the United States before the civil war can be described as such a system. "System maintaining compromises of 1820 and 1850 were thrashed out in the congress. In view of the cultural differences among north and south the autonomy of the states and the importance of the congress as an arena of elite accommodation, one can readily argue that ante-bellum America was a semi-consociational, if not a consociational, democracy." (p. 19). Two things need to be pointed out. First of all, the two compromises did not hold: the American Civil War erupted ten years after the second compromise. Secondly, one could ask whether they were, in fact, examples of elite accommodation. Both compromises , and the events leading up to them, involved much popular participation: the debates and negotiations were out in the open, and the key figures were at all times aware of, and responsive to, popular opinion. By contrast, Lijphart stresses the secrecy of elite accommodation, its isolation from mass participation, and the ability of elites to keep their constituencies under control.

In Canada, many governmental activities, particularly those concerning intergovernmental relations, are clothed in secrecy. Simeon (1972) stressed the way parliamentary institutions at both the provincial and federal levels act to insulate elites from their mass publics, allowing political elites considerable scope to develop policy and bargain with other governments. Furthermore, there is evidence that Canadian elites in the past have made use of this power to engage in "nation-saving" activities. If we examine the behaviour of Canadian political leaders, particularly provincial and federal leaders in the context of federal-provincial negotiations, one can discern practices which approximate Lijphart's criteria that elites must be aware that if they fail to co-operate then the whole system might collapse. In the early 1960's, a number of provincial premiers really thought that if concessions to Quebec were not made, then the Canadian federation was in severe danger. For example, the premiers of the English-language provinces agreed to Quebec's having its own version of the Canada Pension Plan. Arrangements for opting out of shared-cost programs in return for block grants can also be seen as concessions to provincial demands in general, and Quebec demands in particular. Many leaders, both provincial and federal, perceived a need for co-operation and concession if Canada was to remain a viable entity.

Noel's analogy between the Netherlands and Canada has something to recommend it. The two countries are close in a number of dimensions, contrary to what McRae and Wolinetz have argued. In Canada, as in the Netherlands, there are distinctive subcultures, and there is a balance in the number of subcultures. Our form of government is highly secretive and elitist in nature: bargaining frequently takes place in secret, for example, and there are other examples of accommodative behaviour ensuring the survival of the system. Does this make Canada a consociational democracy then? No, not quite, unfortunately.

In the Netherlands, the blocs judge their importance in terms of relative size, and none of them claims special status. Public goods are distributed among the blocs on a proportional basis. The difference with Canada is evident. Over time, Quebec has argued vigorously for the two nation thesis, for special status, and now for sovereignty-association.[10] Other provinces, too, have argued for special treatment, and this has enormously complicated the game of federal-provincial diplomacy. Then too, there is the problem of territoriality, which has two important aspects. The blocs in the Netherlands cannot carve out a piece of territory and call themselves independent countries: this places a major restriction on their behaviour. In Canada this is a possibility, and a province like Quebec has considerably more political resources. Furthermore, the fact of territory makes the allocation of resources much more difficult. There may be several reasons why one province should get more in the way of financial resources, for example, than another. A province can argue that difficulties of terrain and lack of population density pose special problems which should result in a larger per capita grant than is given to some other province (Graham, 1963); the criteria for allocation become much more complex, which, in turn, makes the bargaining process more difficult.

The French-English cleavage and the territorial dimension make Canada quite different from the Netherlands in this respect. What perhaps can be said is not that accommodative practices by Canadian elites have been lacking, but rather that the problems at issue are much more difficult to resolve in Canada than in the Netherlands. There, issues related to the blocs can often be resolved by allocating state funds on a proportional basis. Conflicts over the distribution of resources between classes or regions might pit the socialist bloc against the liberals; but with the Catholics and Protestants these issues would have to be resolved internally, since their memberships cut across both classes and regions. Any policy favouring a particular class, for example, would hurt or benefit Catholics, Protestants, and non-religious blocs in roughly equal fashion. Catholic political leaders were quite scrupulous in ensuring that Catholics did not receive more than their fair share (Bakvis, 1978). In Canada, the opposite is often the case. Many provinces demand, and frequently receive, special treatment. The fact that this is possible probably testifies to the robustness of Canadian political institutions. Thus, if Canada is seen as a consociational democracy, one could argue that in some sense it is even more successful than the Netherlands in view of the special difficulties which have to be surmounted.

D. Consociationalism in Canada: Part II

Noel's view of the provinces as blocs similar to those in the Netherlands, is one way of seeing Canada as a consociational democracy. There are other ways, too. Another group of political scientists see the French-English cleavage as the basic line of cleavage which has been bridged by elites using the consociational method: the provinces are not seen as important factors. Thus, White, Millar and Gagne (1971) in "Political Integration in Quebec During the 1960's", note: "We would suggest that Canadian federation, in particular French-English relations, can be viewed as a consociational democracy which has been faltering for some time." (p. 57). Although it may be fair to say that the French-English division is the most critical line of cleavage in Canada, one should not think that this has given rise to only two basic subcultures: territorial and institutional dimensions cut across this basic line of cleavage; a number of provinces do contain significant numbers of French-Canadians; and in Quebec there is a large group of English-Canadians. The interests of all of these separate groupings are fairly distinct and are often at variance with one another. Again, this makes the Canadian situation much more complicated.

Nevertheless, if one wishes to see consociationalism with French-Canada and English-Canada as the major components, then federal institutions like parliament and cabinet are the most likely arenas for accommodation, and the subcultures would, in all probability, be territorially based. The English-language provinces would cease to be distinct and separate actors: all regional interests in English-Canada would have to be aggregated and articulated through one agency, for example, a political party. By implication, the federal-provincial conference, which gives full status to English-language provinces, would no longer be important. Given the diverging interests between French-Canadians within and without Quebec, it would be unrealistic to expect any single political agency to represent the interests of all French-Canadians regardless of residence[11] – hence, the territorial basis of the subcultures.

In such an arrangement, it would be possible to have political parties drawing support from both solitudes. Accommodation would then take place within the political parties. However, in the examples of Austria, Belgium, and the Netherlands, accommodation takes place *between* political parties, particularly between party leaders, and not *within* political parties. In the case of intra-party accommodation, of which the Canadian brokerage model is the best example, important lines of cleavage are bridged within parties and downplayed at election time. In the case of inter-party accommodation, an important feature of the consociational democracies just mentioned, parties are based on important lines of cleavage, and at election time the parties deliberately try to politicize them. Afterwards, accommodation between party leaders takes place. In this respect, intra-party accommodation deviates from the consociational model.

One possible Canadian scenario which would fulfill the criteria of consociationalism, including inter-party accommodation, would involve distinct political parties from French- and English-Canada, the leaders of which would come together to form coalition cabinets. It is important that a single agency represent the interests of each subculture, and that each subculture support their single agency, otherwise you would have a variation of the problem cited by Noel (1974): a conflict between competing elites within the same subculture. This would be the case if you had two parties competing within Quebec, for example, and would result in rendering more uncertain the outcome of conflicts between subcultures.

This is one model of Canada as a consociational democracy involving accommodation between English and French. Insofar as it requires the downplaying of both regional interests and the importance of provincial governments within English-Canada, and the development of political parties based on language, this model is unlikely to become a reality.

There is another model, based on the notion of homogeneous English and French subcultures, which is probably as pure an elite accommodation model as one can find — sovereignty-association. This proposal entails complete separation of the two language groups. Each would have their own institutions and rules for resolving internal subcultural conflict, as well as a very limited set of institutions for negotiating common problems between the leaders of the two groups. In many ways this is a more plausible model because sovereignty-association sees the current Quebec provincial government (e.g., the legislature, the executive, the civil service, and other provincial jurisdictions) as the appropriate agency to handle French-Canadian interests. Historically, Quebeckers of French descent have looked to their provincial government for protection and help, more so, in fact, than Canadians in other provinces.

The details and feasibility of sovereignty-association are discussed elsewhere.[12] What should be noted here is that many who favour a consociational solution, basically involving French-Canada and

English-Canada as the two actors, implicitly have in mind the sovereignty-association formula. Furthermore, if sovereignty-association were to prove unworkable, we would then have two separate nations. The territorial dimension is again what distinguishes Canada from other consociational countries. When two groups occupy a common territory, elites may have no alternative to co-operation, other than civil violence. With easily separable territories, however, a further option becomes available — separation, and nation status for each group.

Given the fact that there are more than two subcultures in Canada, it is difficult to foresee Canada as a consociational democracy consisting of only two subcultures, based in English- and French-Canada, respectively. This is far too simplistic. If, for analytical purposes, one focuses on the French-English cleavage, it might be better to do so in the context of nineteenth-century Canada. Some see the Province of Canada from 1840 to 1867 as a kind of consociational democracy, where English and French resided together in what was at least nominally a common territory.[13] There developed a system of double Prime Ministership and twin ministerial portfolios, which were carefully balanced to give equal weight to the eastern and western sections of the United Province. Parallel departmental structures were set up, and even the provincial capital rotated at intervals from one section to the other. Both sections developed a two-party system, and each of the four parliamentary groups worked primarily in loose connection with its counter-part in the other section; lower Canada "Bleus" with Upper Canada Conservatives, and lower Canada "Rouges" with Upper Canada Reformers. Thus, consociational democracy during the period of the Province of Canada is usually seen in terms of co-operation between the two linguistic blocs. What should not be neglected, however, is that there were not two, but four, blocs. Moreover, I would question whether relations between French and English can be described in terms of consociationalism. In fact, it is more appropriate to describe the relations between religious groupings in these terms.

In Lower Canada, the Bleus and Rouges represented two basic groups in Quebec society: one represented the Church, the other liberal and anti-clerical forces in Quebec. In Upper Canada, there were also two blocs. Conservatives were generally Protestant and conservative,while Liberals drew considerable support from Catholics. In many ways, the primary line of cleavage during this period was religion and not language. The 1840's saw extensive Irish immigration, and this resulted in a substantial population of English-speaking Catholics. Religious issues were intensified by the importation to Canada of the quarrels between Orangemen and Irish Catholics,and by the Catholic Church's counter-attack on Liberalism during the Papacy of Pope Pius IX. The second half of the 19th Century witnessed more politics of religious confrontation, and this remained an important line of cleavage at the federal level for many years to come. Kenneth McRae (1974b) mentions a book published in 1872, *Political Standing of Irish Catholics in Canada*, whose author stated: "I shall divide the whole population comfortably into two great religious sections, Catholics and Protestants, for all other distinctions seem minor in comparison." (p. 242).

A good deal of institutional segmentation took place during this period. Catholics, for example, acquired not only publicly-supported parochial schools but also a whole network of colleges, newspapers, hospitals, and charitable and welfare institutions. The Catholic population constituted an important subculture in its own right. Protestants lacked the hierarchical organization of the Catholic Church — Protestantism is more democratic and decentralized — but they provided a solid basis of support for the Conservatives, and later for the Progressive Conservative Party. Linguistic issues arose from time to time, but the primary line of cleavage during this period was religion, which thus had considerable influence in structuring the nature of Canadian politics. The Catholic Church, like the Church in the Netherlands, had a high degree of control over its flock, and therefore was able to prevent many issues from becoming politicized: demands were often made in terms of religion rather than language. This was essentially the situation until the early 1960's. What should be stressed is that after 1867 accommodation occurred within political parties, rather than between parties. This would be true also of the period 1840-1867, if one concedes that the Bleus and Tories were more or less a Conservative Party in embryo.

If we want to explain the breakdown in French-English relations in the 1960's, and to explain the rise of problems in the Canadian federation generally, we must see it at least partially in terms of a decline in the religious issue and a rise in the language issue. The language issue, furthermore, has been a lot more intractible than religion was. McRae (1974b) noted that the pattern of institutional segmentation appears to be shifting from religion to language. Evidence for this can be found in many sectors. Schools are increasingly becoming segmented on a linguistic basis. In English-Canada, private French-speaking Catholic high schools have entered the public system. Health care has become a public responsibility, more organized on linguistic lines. The media, particularly radio and television, have become segmented more and more along linguistic lines (McRae, 1974b, p. 243).

McRae notes that this shift in patterns of segmentation away from religion and towards language has had distinct political consequences: it has narrowed the basis of segmentation in English-language provinces and broadened it in Quebec. Another factor contributing to the breakdown of relations between French-Canada and the rest of Canada is that, in the past, the French-English cleavage was characterized by geographic separation. Even where there was propinquity, substantial occupational differentiation tended to keep the groups apart (McRae, 1974b, p. 244). In many ways, institutional segmentation of the French-English cleavage was not really necessary. Now that the language issue has become much more salient, it has also become more difficult to control, given the lack of appropriate institutions.

Canada is not alone in this. In Belgium there are two language groups, but it was not until after the second World War that the language issue became salient. As in Canada, this cleavage has resulted in conflict which does not lend itself readily to compromise. Leaders of the groups pushing language issues have not been able to control their followers. There have been riots, the behaviour of linguistic parties in the Belgian parliament has been highly unstable, and electoral support for these parties has fluctuated considerably. The consociational model is much more appropriate to societies where the basic lines of cleavage are based on organization, where the subcultures are organizational rather than ethnic or linguistic, and where they cut across major current economic issues. The religious cleavage lends itself more readily to a type of politics which is much less virulent than politics based on ethnic or linguistic differences.

This is not to say that linguistically-divided societies are, *ipso facto*, unstable. What the lessons of the United Provinces, Belgium before the early 1960's, and Switzerland boil down to is that political stability requires the depoliticization of the language issue. Institutions like supreme courts may take language differences into account, but in the above examples, language is not a basis for organized political activity, such as movements and parties. In Switzerland, constitutional powers affecting language are largely in the hands of the Cantons. The national political parties do not appeal on the basis of language. The Swiss Catholic Conservative party, for example, draws support from German, French, and Italian speakers (Obler et al, 1977). Proportional representation by language, mutual veto power, and even special privileges for minority groups, are more or less taken for granted, and are not subjects for intense negotiation, particularly not at election time. A true consociational democracy deals with politically-active cleavage patterns. In the Netherlands, political leaders deliberately urged people to vote according to their religion/ideology, and most people did: party leaders reconciled their differences after the election and proceeded to rule in collegial fashion for another four or five years.

Unfortunately, inter-party accommodation is not always possible in a linguistically-divided society. Leaders of linguistic parties may well be successful in using the politics of language to gain support, but they may also find themselves unable to control that support. The fires of linguistic conflict are easy to start, but difficult to quench. As Brian Barry (1975) notes: "Ethnic conflict is a conflict of solidary groups (which) do not need organization to work up a riot or a program so long as they have some way of recognizing who belongs to which group ... Unlike ethnic segments, religious and ideological segments are defined in terms of organizations and by the fact that they follow certain leaders; as a result the leaders can count on the loyal support of their followers for agreements that they make with the leaders of rival segments." (Quoted in Lijphart, 1977a, p. 231). In short, the consociational model is frequently unworkable where ethnicity or language is the basis for political conflict: elites from the different blocs frequently are not in a position to make agreements which would be binding on their followers.

E. Lessons?

What are the implications? If one favours consociationalism, one makes sure that the subcultures involved in the consociational solution are based on organization rather than on natural solidarity groups. This would rule out consociational schemes which highlight differences between the two language groups. What kind of organizations? I have drawn a parallel between the blocs in the Netherlands and the provinces in Canada which, as Cairns (1977) has suggested, have grown largely as a result of institutions, constitutional interpretation, and leadership. The strength of the former derives from the rules of the game and the talents of political entrepreneurs. It was also illustrated that institutions and institutional boundaries in Canada have the effect of creating a number of linguistic minorities who feel themselves aggrieved, and of reinforcing one very large natural solidarity group (French-Canadians in Quebec) who have a strong sense of grievance. Nevertheless, it can be argued that the provinces are the closest we have to the blocs or pillars of the smaller West European democracies. Furthermore, it could be argued that the provinces and provincial identities are now so strongly rooted that it is better to recognize them and to institutionalize them even further. Most proposals calling for the strengthening of the provinces also call for direct provincial governmental representation at the centre. This kind of intra-state federalism, as noted earlier, would reinforce and institutionalize the federal-provincial conference, making it the primary body for policy-making in Canada. Many people expect, or hope, that accommodation will take place within this body. Should this happen, then Canada could be called a consociational democracy. Given the numerous proposals promoting this kind of arrangement, in addition to the demands for decentralization by the provinces, this is by far the most plausible scenario.

I would, however, argue strongly against proposals which would, consciously or unconsciously, promote a vision of this kind. Many proposals calling for decentralization, particularly provincial schemes stressing the water-tight compartments approach (i.e., disentanglement), call not so much for elite co-operation as for elite autonomy. There is no guarantee that elites from the provinces will co-operate. One can cite examples of federal-provincial co-operation in the 1960's, but one is hard-pressed to do so in the 1970's, with the possible exception of the Anti-Inflation Board agreement in 1975. Overall, this is not a promising harbinger for the future. Even if there is co-operation, a major problem with consociationalism, an arrangement so dependent on elites operating in secrecy, is that a change in elite attitudes can have a major impact, even without corresponding changes in society.

Next, the question is whether we want to institutionalize further and legitimize provincial governments whose power and base of popular support may wane in the future. Today, Canadians appear to be favourably disposed towards their provincial governments. In future years, however, they may turn back to the federal government for help, particularly English-Canadians, and find that it is no longer able to act alone in a particular area. Provincial governments are probably not as artificial as some have depicted them, but there is considerable danger of entrenching institutional self-interests in any kind of formalized consociational arrangement. It is noteworthy that in the Netherlands during the 1960's, the most cohesive and enduring subculture, the Catholic bloc, suddenly began to crumble, so that by the 1970's, it played a much less important role than before. Dutch Catholics decided that when it came to politics, religion was no longer important. Unfortunately, in Canada with regard to the provinces, citizens may not have such direct control if the role of provincial governments in federal policy-making is institutionalized.

This brings us to the third reason for rejecting consociationalism as a vehicle for integration in the Canadian context. Consociationalism requires secrecy. Lijphart stressed this. The rank-and-file of the subcultures should not question their leaders about the bargains arrived at with the other subcultures. Leaders must create a certain distance between themselves and their followers. Given the current Canadian climate of mistrust in the machinery and processes of government decision-making, it would not be possible to fulfill these criteria. Currently, a host of minor decisions by governments are made in secret, and they are not always well-received when they become known. No longer can major constitutional change be made privately between federal and provincial leaders: public constraints on them are great, and some form of public legitimation of political agreements seems inevitable.

Lijphart (1975) noted that consociationalism in the Netherlands began to break down precisely when the tenets concerning government secrecy began to be questioned during the late 1960's. In Canada, there are likely to be more, rather than fewer, demands for openness in government and increased public participation, and this would not be conducive to adopting further consociational practices. As Noel (1974) notes: "... a decline of 'elitism' in Canada and its replacement by a general accept-ance of the Jacksonian myth of popular or 'participatory' democracy may be detrimental to the maintenance of Canadian federalism if it leads to a situation in which the mass of the people are unwilling to accept the inter-elite accommodations made by their political leaders." (p. 267). This, to some extent, may be the case already. Beginning in the late 1960's, one can see less accommodation taking place between first minis-ters, as compared with the situation in the earlier part of that decade. This coincides with an increase in the publicity given to first ministers' conferences, particularly constitutional conferences. Currently, these conferences are covered extensively by the media, usually with a buildup of publicity occurring some weeks before the actual event. The provincial premiers and the prime minister are expected to state publicly their positions beforehand. With television penetrating even into the sup-posedly closed meetings, the actors, supported by extensive staffs, are rarely in a position to deviate from their stated positions and to arrive at compromise solutions. Again, there is very little likelihood of these conferences becoming more anonymous in the future.

What are the alternatives? I would like to see political organizations which stress functional issues and downplay those related to ethno-nationalism. Ironically, the only organizations in Canada which offer this potential are the national political parties. Noel (1974) dismissed assumptions concerning the role of parties in achieving national integra-tion as dubious (p. 268). Cairns (1968) critically evaluated the notion of brokerage politics and showed that Canadian political parties really have not acted in this capacity. In Noel's case, one can say that he does discuss the importance of parties, if only indirectly — (how did former External Affairs Minister Don Jamieson move himself from Newfoundland to Ottawa? Answer: via the Liberal party). As for the brokerage theory — in the past, economic issues (tariffs, the national policy) and religious issues have allowed the major parties to find support from both solitudes and from the different regions. This occurred in spite of the fact that the electoral system provided incentives for racial and regional appeals, which the parties, on occasion, have taken advantage of (Cairns, 1968; Lovink, 1970). The shift in cleavage patterns discussed earlier, combined with the effects of the electoral system, has exacerbated this problem.

How do we encourage brokerage politics? A first and preliminary step would be to change the electoral system to include a large element of proportional representation along the lines suggested by William Irvine (1979). This is only a preliminary step, however. The decline of the Canadian party system in representing regional interests is due only partially to the electoral system. Many political leaders find life at the provincial level much more attractive. As Smiley (1976) documents, in recent decades fewer and fewer provincial politicians have shifted to the federal level, and provincial and federal party organizations have grown apart.

Proportional representation may help revitalize the party system by moving it closer to the brokerage politics model. Additional incentives are needed, however, to draw talent and political clout from the regions to Ottawa, and to have these people develop a commitment to the national interest, as opposed to strictly regional interests. These incentives are most likely to be found in the realm of patronage and in the disbursement of public funds generally. Secondly, positions of power and influence at the centre should be opened up and distributed more widely. Parliamentary committees should be given more power through greater use of green papers and pre-legislative hearings, and the government should pay greater heed to committee proposals in drafting the actual proposals. Hans Lovink (1973) discussed the benefits of such reforms, as well as improving the quality of legistators and their education, public participation, and the like. By implication, it would make participation in federal politics more attractive, and thus strengthen the centre.

A less direct, but still important, way to strengthen the centre would be to apply the rule of proportionality to appointments made to regulatory boards and agencies. Appointments would be made in terms of regions by the national political parties in proportion to the percentage of the vote obtained by them. Potential appointees would have to work through the federal political parties, and the parties, in turn, would have to pay attention to regional representation. Not much imagination and ingenuity is required to think of further schemes to enhance the power and attractiveness of the centre.

The strategy of revitalizing the centre is not a panacea. Conflicts concerning language are not going to disappear overnight, but will continue to be the focus of political discussion. It is no easy task to depoliticize the language issue without removing, or at least minimizing, the sense of grievance. It can be argued that French-Canada, at least in Quebec, has the tools available (for example, the legislation outlined in Bill 101), to ensure equal chances for occupational mobility and the survival of the French language. One can argue further that what is needed is time to allow these changes to have a demonstrative effect. A further suggestion might be to "federalize" the federal government even more through administrative decentralization. Recent changes in the Department of Regional Economic Expansion (DREE) offers one such example. The Quebec section of DREE operates virtually autonomously, although policies are co-ordinated in Ottawa. The CBC might be a further example. What should be stressed is that this kind of decentralization does not imply giving more power to the provinces. Control would remain in Ottawa, but more effort would be made by the centre to sink regional roots, essentially by-passing the provinces, though not necessarily undermining their authority.

In summary, a good case can be made to strengthen the centre by transforming the party system with the intent to make the parties brokers of regional and economic interests. This stretegy is implied in William Riker's *Federalism: Origin, Operation, Significance*, where he stresses the important role party systems play in integrating federal systems. As noted earlier, Riker's argument has been criticized for attaching too much importance to the effect of party systems, and for saying that the success of parties in integrating federal systems depends, in turn, on a lot of other factors. It was pointed out that other institutions and organizations may act as integrative forces. In Canada, however, the party system seems to be the only mechanism available for for politicizing socioeconomic issues and for depoliticising the language cleavage. The consociational model, whether based on two segments (English-French), or on ten segments (provinces), involves politicizing the language cleavage and sharpening distinctly regional issues, something which should be avoided.

In the Netherlands, consociationalism involving sharply defined subcultures has been successful in the past because: a) leaders could operate in relative secrecy; b) the issues separating the different blocs were relatively narrow ones, and a consensus prevailed on basic issues; and c) there was a consensus and co-operation not only at the elite level, but also at the mass level, which helped with public acceptance of elite co-operation and toleration of policy outcomes. These conditions do not prevail in Canada. It is unrealistic to expect problems at the national level to be resolved by consensus of a very narrow elite. It is better to develop a commitment to difficult decisions on a broader level involving local elites and ordinary citizens, as well as national and provincial leaders. Such commitment is much more likely to occur within the framework of popularly-based national parties than within the narrow confines of federal-provincial conferences.

Footnotes

1. One might add that certain practices which are considered by some to be consociational are, in fact, not, insofar as certain features, (e.g., distinctive subcultures) are lacking. This will become evident later in the paper.

2. As Wolinetz (1978) points out, elite accommodation is a feature of virtually all democratic societies. Elite accommodation in itself would not necessarily indicate that the system in question is consociational in nature. Consociational democracy involves dissensus at the mass level and accommodative behaviour on the part of the leaders of conflicting groups. Such behaviour can be classified as consociational practice. One can also label consociational elite behaviour which ensures control over their followers and/or enforces the rules of secrecy.

3. What these diverging goals and interests are has never been spelled out by Lijphart (1968) in the case of the Netherlands. One goal of the blocs would be maintaining cultural distinctiveness and integrity, but this would not necessarily result in conflict. Elsewhere, Lijphart (1977a) indicates that, in the case of developing societies, the goal of ethnic groups is often dominance over other groups, but that conflict can be averted through consociational means.

4. See Daalder, 1974a, 1974b; Barry, 1975; McRae, 1974b; Obler *et al*, 1977.

5. Particularly after World War II, the Socialist and Catholic trade union federations converged in the areas of services and wage demands. In 1976, the two organizations came together to form a Catholic/socialist trade union federation.

6. For a detailed discussion of these changes, see Wolinetz (1973).

7. The Catholic Church was aided by relatively late industrialization in the Netherlands. Catholic priests could see what had happened in countries like Britain, France, and Germany, and they acted accordingly.

8. The Saskatchewan Progressive Conservative Party said that although the NDP government had made errors in its legislation, it was supporting the government because it was pro-Saskatchewan and anti-Ottawa. The provincial Liberal Party, which supported Ottawa, lost all its seats in the 1978 provincial election. (See Paus-Jensen, 1979).

9. Cairns (1979) notes that there are two variants of intra-state, as opposed to inter-state, federalism. One variant features direct provincial government representation in the central policy-making process, the other was regional and linguistic representation through such mechanisms as the federal parties, a revised Senate with regional representatives appointed by the federal parties or the federal government (e.g., Bill C-60). I think, however, that Cairns glosses over the distinction between the two. The former would dilute the centre and come closer to the consociational model. The latter, if the strategy works, would help revitalize the central government by getting regional representatives to develop a commitment to central institutions and, therefore, would not be incompatible with inter-state federalism. (See also Smiley, 1971).

10. It should be stressed that the demands by Quebec for special status can be seen as quite justifiable, since, over the long run, French-Canadians received considerably less than a proportionate share of many of the benefits disbursed by the federal government (e.g., civil service positions); and, of course, their unique cultural-linguistic identity adds legitimacy to their claims.

11. Historically, French-Canadians in Quebec have opted for protection of Quebec's integrity if a trade-off had to be made between protecting French-Canadians outside of Quebec by means of the federal government or minimizing federal government

interference in the affairs of Quebec. Thus, French-Canadians outside of Quebec would have to find protection from their provincial government, the federal government, or English-Canadian political parties, rather than from Quebec politicians.

12. See Leslie (1979); Pentland and Soberman (forthcoming).

13. See the articles by McRae, Ormsby, and Stanley in the McRae (1974a) volume.

Bibliography

Albinski, H.S. (1973) Canadian and Australian Politics in Comparative Perspective. New York: Oxford University Press.

Bakvis, H. (1978) "Electoral Stability and Electoral Change: The Case of the Catholic Party in the Netherlands." Ph.D. diss., University of British Columbia.

Barry, Brian (1975) "Political Accommodation and Consociational Democracy," British Journal of Political Science 5:477-505.

Bendix, R. (1967) "Tradition and Modernity Reconsidered," Comparative Studies in Society and History 9:292-346.

Birch, A.H. (1967) "Approaches to the Study of Federalism," in A. Wildavsky (ed.) American Federalism in Perspective. Boston: Little, Brown and Company, pp. 59-77.

———— (1955) Federalism, Finance, and Social Legislation in Canada, Australia and the United States. Oxford: Clarendon Press.

Bird, R.M. (1970) The Growth of Government Spendings in Canada. Canadian Tax Papers no. 51. Toronto: Canadian Tax Foundation.

Black, C. (1977) Duplessis. Toronto: McClelland and Stewart.

Black, E.R. (1975) Divided Loyalties: Canadian Concepts of Federalism. Montreal and London: McGill-Queen's University Press.

Blake, D.E. (1972) "The Measurement of Regionalism in Canadian Voting Patterns," Canadian Journal of Political Science. 5:55-81.

Bottomore, T. (1965) Classes in Modern Society. London: Allen and Unwin.

Breton, A. and Scott, A. (1978) The Economic Constitution of Federal States. Toronto: University of Toronto Press.

Breugel, J.W. (1973) "The Germans in Pre-War Czechoslovakia," pp. 167-187 in V. Mametey and R. Luza (eds.) A History of the Czechoslovak Republic 1918-1948. Princeton, N.J.: Princeton University Press.

Buchanan, J. and G. Tullock (1962) The Calculus of Consent: Logical Foundations of Constitutional Democracy. Ann Arbor: University of Michigan Press.

Burnham, W.D. (1972) "Political Immunization and Political Confessionalism," Journal of Interdisciplinary History 3:1-30.

Cairns, A.C. (1971) "The Judicial Committee and Its Critics," Canadian Journal of Political Science. 4:301-45.

—— (1977) "The Governments and Societies of Canadian Federalism." Canadian Journal of Political Science 10:695-725.

—— (1979) From Interstate to Intrastate Federalism in Canada. Kingston: Institute of Intergovernmental Relations.

—— (1968) "The Electoral System and the Party System in Canada." Canadian Journal of Political Science 1:55-80.

Canada Task Force on Canadian Unity (1979) A Future Together: Observations and Recommendations. Hull: Supply and Services.

Careless, Anthony (1977) Initiative and Response: The Adaption of Canadian Federalism to Regional Economic Development. Montreal: McGill-Queen's University Press.

Carter, G.E. (1971) Canadian Conditional Grants Since World War II. Toronto: Canadian Tax Foundation.

Connor, W. (1977) "Ethnonationalism in the First World: The Present in Historical Perspective." in M. Esman (ed.) Ethnic Conflict in the Western World. Ithaca: Cornell University Press.

Cook, R. (1968) "The Manitoba School Question in the Context of Confederation," in L. Clark (ed.) The Manitoba School Question: Majority Rule or Minority Rights. Toronto: Copp Clark.

Corry, J.A. and J.E. Hodgetts (1959) Democratic Government and Politics. Toronto: University of Toronto Press.

Daalder, H. (1966) "The Netherlands: Opposition in a Segmented Society," pp. 188-236 in R. Dahl (ed.) Political Oppositions in Western Democracies. New Haven: Yale University Press.

—— (1974a) "On Building Consociational Nations: The Cases of the Netherlands and Switzerland," pp. 107-24 in K. McRae (ed.) Consociational Democracy. Toronto: McClelland and Stewart.

—— (1974b) "The Consociational Democracy Theme." World Politics 26:604-21.

Davis, Rufus (1967) "The 'Federal Principle' Reconsidered," pp. 3-32 in A. Wildavsky (ed.) American Federalism in Perspective. Boston: Little, Brown and Company.

Dawson, R.M. (1970) The Government of Canada, rev. by N. Ward. Toronto: University of Toronto Press.

Deutsch, K.W. et al (1957) Political Community and the North Atlantic Area. Princeton: Princeton University Press.

—— (1975) "The Political Significance of Linguistic Conflicts," pp. 7-28 in J.G. Savard and R. Vigneault (eds.) Multilingual Political Systems. Quebec: Les Presses de l'Université Laval.

Duchacek, I.D. (1970) Comparative Federalism: The Territorial Dimension of Politics. Toronto: Holt, Rinehart and Winston.

—— (1973) "External and Internal Challenge to the Federal Bargain." Paper prepared for the Conference on "The Politics of Intergovernmental Relations in Federal Systems: Urban Perspectives." Philadelphia: Center for the Study of Federalism and the Urban Studies Center, Temple University.

Dogan, M. (1967) "Political Cleavage and Social Stratification in France and Italy," pp. 129-98 in S.M. Lipset and S. Rokkan (eds.) Party Systems and Voter Alignments. New York: The Free Press.

Dunn, J.A. (1972) "Consociational Democracy and Language Conflict: A Comparison of the Belgian and Swiss Experiences." Comparative Political Studies 5:9-16.

Elazar, D. (1962) The American Partnership. Chicago: University of Chicago Press.

Elkins, D. and R. Simeon (1980) Small Worlds: Provinces and Parties in Canadian Political Life. Toronto: Methuen.

Ellemers, J. (1967) "The Revolt of the Netherlands: The Part Played by Religion." Social Compass 14:167-203.

Enloe, Cynthia (1973) Ethnic Conflict and Political Development. Boston: Little, Brown and Company.

Esman, M. (1977) "Scottish Nationalism, North Sea Oil, and the British Response," pp. 251-286 in M. Esman (ed.) Ethnic Conflict in the Western World. Ithaca: Cornell University Press.

Falardeau, J.C. (1964) "The Role and Importance of the Church in French Canada," pp. 342-57 in M. Rioux and Y. Martin (eds.) French Canadian Society, Vol. 1. Toronto: McClelland and Stewart.

Flanz, G. (1968) "The West Indies," pp. 91-124 in T. Franck (ed.) Why Federations Fail. London: University of London Press.

Fogarty, M.P. (1957) Christian Democracy in Western Europe 1820-1953. Notre Dame: Notre Dame University Press.

Frank, A.G. (1969) Capitalism and Underdevelopment in Latin America. New York: Monthly Review Press.

Friedrich, Carl (1973) "Corporate Federalism and Linguistic Politics," paper presented to the International Political Science Association IXth World Congress, Montreal.

Furtado, C. (1967) Obstacles to Development in Latin America. New York: Anchor Books.

Furnivall, J.S. (1939) Netherlands India: A Study of Plural Economy. Cambridge: Cambridge University Press.

Gadourek, I. (1956) A Dutch Community: Social and Cultural Structure and Process in a Bulb-growing Region in the Netherlands. Leiden: Stenferr Kroese.

Geertz, C. (1963) "The Integrative Revolution: Primordial Sentiments and Civil Politics in the New States," pp. 105-57 in C. Geertz (ed.) Old Societies and New States. New York: The Free Press.

Gordon, H. and N. Gordon (1974) Austrian Empire: Abortive Federation. New York: Heath.

Graham, J. (1963) Fiscal Adjustment and Economic Development. Toronto: University of Toronto Press.

Greenwood, G. (1976) The Future of Australian Federalism. 2nd ed. St. Lucia: University of Queensland Press.

Guindon, H. (1964) "Social Unrest, Social Class and Quebec's Bureaucratic Revolution," Queen's Quarterly 71:150-62.

Hamilton, R. (1965) "Affluence and the Worker: The West German Case," American Journal of Sociology 71:144-152.

——— (1967) Affluence and the French Worker in the Fourth Republic. Princeton: Princeton University Press.

Hechter, M. (1977) Internal Colonialism: The Celtic Fringe in British National Development, 1536-1966. Berkeley: University of California Press.

Henig, S. (1969) European Political Parties. New York: Praeger.

Hirschman, A.O. (1970) Exit, Voice and Loyalty: Responses to Decline in Firms, Organizations and States. Cambridge: Harvard University Press.

Hoggart, R. (1967) The Uses of Literacy: Changing Patterns in British Mass Culture. London: Chatto and Windus.

Horowitz, G. (1972) "Conservatism, Liberalism and Socialism in Canada: An Interpretation," pp. 78-96 in H. Thorburn (ed.) Party Politics in Canada. 3rd ed. Toronto: Prentice-Hall.

——— (1968) Canadian Labour in Politics. Toronto: University of Toronto Press.

Hutcheson, J. (1978) Dominance and Dependency: Liberalism and National Policies in the North Atlantic Triangle. Toronto: McClelland and Stewart.

Innis, H. (1950) Empire and Communications. Toronto: University of Toronto Press.

Irvine, William (1979) Does Canada Need a New Electoral System? Kingston: Institute of Intergovernmental Relations.

Kann, R. (1950) The Multinational Empire: Nationalism and National Reform in the Habsburg Monarchy 1848-1918. New York: Columbia University Press.

Kerr, C. and J. Siegel (1964) "The Interindustry Propensity to Strike: An International Comparison," pp. 105-147 in C. Kerr (ed.) Labor and Management in Industrial Society. Garden City: Doubleday.

Knopff, R. (1979) "Language and Culture in the Canadian Debate: The Battle of the White Papers," Canadian Review of Studies in Nationalism 6:66-82.

Kruijt, J.P. (1974) "The Netherlands: The Influence of Denominationalism on Social Life and Organizational Patterns," pp. 128-36 in K. McRae (ed.) Consociational Democracy. Toronto: McClelland and Stewart.

Kwavnick, D. (1968) "French Canadians and the Civil Service of Canada." Canadian Public Administration 11:97-112.

——— ed. and intro. (1973) The Tremblay Report: Report of the Royal Commission of Inquiry on Constitutional Problems. The Carleton Library No. 64. Toronto: McClelland and Stewart.

La Fédération des francophones hors Quebec (1979) Face to Face with a Failing Country: A New Association for the Two Founding Peoples. Ottawa.

LaPalombara, J. (1970) "Parsimony and Empiricism and Comparative Politics: An Anti-Scholastic View," pp. 123-49 in R. Holt and J. Turner, (eds.) The Methodology of Comparative Research. New York: The Free Press.

Laponce, J. (1960) "The Protection of Minorities." Berkeley: University of California Press.

Leih, G.H. (1962) Kaart van Politiek Nederland. Kampen: Jilt Kok.

Leslie, P. (1979) "Equal to Equal: Economic Association and the Canadian Common Market," Kingston: Institute of Intergovernmental Relations.

Levin, M. (1970) "Fission and Fusion on the French Left," Ph.D. Diss., Cornell University.

Levitt, Kari (1970) Silent Surrender. Toronto: MacMillan.

Lijphart, A. (1974) "Consociational Democracy," pp. 70-89 in K.D. McRae (ed.) Consociational Democracy. Toronto: McClelland and Stewart.

——— (1975) "The Politics of Accommodation: Pluralism and Democracy in the Netherlands" 2nd ed. Berkeley: University of California Press.

——— (1977a) Democracy in Plural Societies. New Haven: Yale University Press.

——— (1977b) "Political Theories and the Explanation of Ethnic Conflict in the Western World: Falsified Predictions and Plausible Postdictions," pp. 46-64 in M. Esman (ed.) Ethnic Conflict in the Western World. Ithaca: Cornell University Press.

Linz, J. (1967) "Cleavage and Consensus in West German Politics: The Early Fifties," pp. 283-321 in S.M. Lipset and S. Rokkan (eds.) Party Systems and Voter Alignments. New York: The Free Press

Lipset, S.M. and S. Rokkan, (1967) "Cleavage Structures, Party Systems, and Voter Alignments," pp. 1-64 in S.M. Lipset and S. Rokkan (eds.) Party Systems and Voter Alignments: Cross-National Perspectives. New York: The Free Press.

——— and R. Bendix, (1964) Social Mobility in Industrial Society. Berkeley: University of California Press.

Livingston, W.S. (1956) Federalism and Constitutional Change. Oxford: Clarendon Press.

Lorwin, V. (1966) "Belgium: Religion, Class, and Language in National Politics," pp. 147-87 in R. Dahl (ed.) Political Oppositions in Western Democracies. New Haven: Yale University Press.

——— (1974) "Segmented Pluralism: Ideological Cleavages and Political Cohesion in the Smaller European Democracies," pp. 33-69 in K. McRae (ed.) Consociational Democracy. Toronto: McClelland and Stewart, pp. 33-69.

Lovink, J.A.A. (1970) "On Analysing the Impact of the Electoral System on the Party System in Canada," Canadian Journal of Political Science 3:497-516.

——— (1973) "Parliamentary Reform and Governmental Effectiveness in Canada." Canadian Public Administration 16:35-54.

Mackenzie, A. and A. Silver (1968) Angels in Marble: Working Class Conservatives in Urban England. Chicago: University of Chicago Press.

MacMillan, C.M. (1978) "Language, Culture and Political Conflict: Some Reflections on the Relationships." Paper presented to the annual meeting of the Canadian Political Science Association, London, Ontario.

MacPherson, C.B. (1953) Democracy in Alberta: Social Credit and the Party System. Toronto: University of Toronto Press.

Mallory, J.R. (1965) "The Five Faces of Federalism," pp. 3-15 in P.A. Crépeau and C.B. Macpherson (eds.) The Future of Canadian Federalism. Toronto: University of Toronto Press.

——— (1954) Social Credit and the Federal Power in Canada. Toronto: University of Toronto Press.

Mathias, P. (1971) Forced Growth. Toronto: Lewis and Samuel.

McRae, K.D. (1973) "Empire, Language and Nation: The Canadian Case," pp. 144-76 in S. Rokkan and S. Eisenstadt (eds.) Building States and Nations. Beverly Hills: Sage.

———— (1974a) "Introduction," pp. 1-27 in K. McRae (ed.) Consociational Democracy. Toronto: McClelland and Stewart.

———— (1974b) "Consociationalism and the Canadian Political System," pp. 238-61 in K. McRae (ed.) Consociational Democracy. Toronto: McClelland and Stewart.

McWhinney, E. (1966) Federal Constitution - Makings for a Multi-National World. Leyden: Sijthoff.

Meisel, J. (1963) "The Stalled Omnibus: Canadian Parties in the 1960's," Social Research 30:367-90.

———— (1973) Working Papers on Canadian Politics, rev. ed. Montreal: McGill-Queen's University Press.

Milne, R.S. (1972) "The Overdeveloped Study of Political Development," Canadian Journal of Political Science 5:560-68

Milner, H. and S.H. Milner (1973) The Decolonization of Quebec: An Analysis of Left-Wing Nationalism. Toronto: McClelland and Stewart.

Morrison, R. (1970) Corporate Adaptibility to Bilingualism. Ottawa: Queen's Printer.

Noel, S.J. (1974) "Consociational Democracy and Canadian Federalism," pp. 262-8 in K. McRae (ed.) Consociational Democracy. Toronto: McClelland and Stewart.

———— (1977a) "Political Parties and Elite Accommodation: Interpretations of Canadian Federalism," pp. 64-83 in J.P. Meekison (ed.) Canadian Federalism: Myth or Reality. 3rd ed. Toronto: Methuen, pp. 64-83.

———— (1977b) "The Prime Minister's Role in a Consociational Democracy," pp. 154-8 in T. Hockin (ed.) Apex of Power. Toronto: Prentice-Hall, pp. 154-8.

Nordlinger, E. (1972) Conflict Regulation in Divided Societies. Cambridge: Center for International Affairs, Harvard University.

Obler, Jeffrey et al (1977) Decision-Making in Smaller Democracies: The Consociational "Burden". Beverly Hills: Sage.

Olson, M. (1976) "The Determinants of Relative Rates of Economic Growth and Possibilities for Redistribution." Unpublished.

———— (1965) The Logic of Collective Action. Cambridge: Harvard University Press.

Options: Proceedings of the Conference on the Future of the Canadian Federation (1977) Toronto: University of Toronto.

Ormsby, William (1974) "The Province of Canada: The Emergence of Consociational Politics," pp. 269-74 in K. McRae (ed.) Consociational Democracy. Toronto: McClelland and Stewart.

Parkin, F. (1971) Class Inequality and Political Order. London: MacGibbon and Kee.

———— (1967) "Working Class Conservatives: A Theory of Political Deviance." British Journal of Sociology 18:278-90.

Paus-Jensen, A. (1979) "Resource Taxation and the Supreme Court of Canada: The Cigol Case." Canadian Public Policy 5:45-58.

Pentland, C. and D. Soberman. International Economic Associations and the Canadian Common Market (tentative). Forthcoming.

Peters, G., J. Doughtie, and M. McCulloch (1977) "Types of Democratic System and Types of Public Policy." Comparative Politics 9:327 355.

Phillips, D. (1978) Interest Groups and Intergovernmental Relations: Language Policy-Making in Canada. Kingston: Institute of Intergovernmental Relations.

———— (1979) "National/Regional Language Planning in Canada: Official Bilingualism and Bill 101." Paper presented to the Canadian Political Science Association Annual Meeting.

Poel, D. (1976) "The Diffusion of Legislation Among the Canadian Provinces: A Statistical Analysis," Canadian Journal of Political Science, 9:605-26.

Porter, J. (1965) The Vertical Mosaic. Toronto: University of Toronto Press.

Presthus, R. (1974) Political Leaders, Bureaucrats and Pressure Groups: Elite Accommodation in Canadian Politics. Toronto: MacMillan.

Przeworski, A. and H. Teune (1970) The Logic of Comparative Social Inquiry. New York: Wiley.

Public Service Commission of Canada (1980) Annual Report. Ottawa.

Quinn, H.F. (1963) The Union Nationale: A Study in Quebec Nationalism. Toronto: University of Toronto Press.

Riker, W.H. (1969) "Six Books in Search of a Subject, or Does Federalism Exist and Does It Matter?" Comparative Politics 2:135-46.

———— (1964) Federalism: Origin, Operation, Significance. Boston: Little, Brown.

Rawkins, P. (1978) "Outsiders as Insiders: The Implications of Minority Nationalism in Scotland and Wales." Comparative Politics 10:141-175.

Rabushka, A. and K. Sheple (1972) Politics in Plural Societies: A Theory of Democratic Instability. Columbus: Merrill.

Rogier, L.J. and N. de Rooy (1953) In Vrijheid Herboren: Katholiek Nederland, 1853-1953. The Hague: Pax.

Rogowski, R. (1974) Rational Legitimacy: A Theory of Political Support. Princeton: Princeton University Press.

———— (1978) "Rationalist Theories of Politics: A Midterm Report." World Politics 30:296-323.

Rose, R. (1968) "Class and Party Divisions: Britain as a Test Case," Sociology 2: 129-62.

———— and D. Urwin (1969) "Social Cohesion, Political Parties and Strains in Regimes," Comparative Political Studies 2:7-67.

Ross, George (1977) "Party and Mass Organization: The Changing Relationship of PCF and CGT," pp. 504-40 in D. Blackmer and S. Tarrow (eds.) Communism in Italy and France. Princeton, N.J.: Princeton University Press.

Rudolph, L. and S. Rudolph (1967) The Modernity of Tradition. Chicago: University of Chicago.

Sayeed, K. (1967) The Political System of Pakistan. Boston: Houghton Mifflin.

Schattschneider, E.E. (1959) The Semi-Sovereign People. New York: Holt, Rhinehart and Winston.

Sen, A.K. (1973) Collective Choice and Social Welfare. San Francisco: Holden-Day.

Shonfield, A. (1965) Modern Capitalism: The Changing Balance of Public and Private Power. London: Oxford University Press.

Simeon, R. (1978) "Criteria for Choice." Paper presented to the Workshop on the Political Economy of Confederation. Ottawa: Economic Council of Canada.

——— (1972) Federal-Provincial Diplomacy: The Making of Recent Policy in Canada. Toronto: University of Toronto Press.

——— (1977) "Regionalism and Canadian Political Institutions," pp. 292-303 in J.P. Meekison (ed.) Canadian Federalism: Myth or Reality? 3rd ed. Toronto: Methuen.

——— and D.J. Elkins (1974) "Regional Political Cultures in Canada," Canadian Journal of Political Science 7:397-437.

Smiley, D.V. (1976) Canada in Question: Federalism in the Seventies, 2nd ed. Toronto: McGraw Hill.

——— (1971) "The Structural Problem of Canadian Federalism," Canadian Public Administration 14:326-43

——— (1970) Constitutional Adaptation and Canadian Federalism Since 1945. Ottawa: Queen's Printer.

Smith, M.G. (1965) The Plural Society in the British West Indies. Berkeley: University of California Press.

Sorokin, P. (1927) Social and Cultural Mobility. Glencoe: The Free Press.

Sproule-Jones, M.H. (1975) Public Choice and Federalism in Australia and Canada. Canberra: Australian National University Press.

Stanley, George (1974) "The Federal Bargain: The Contractarian Basis of Confederation," pp. 275-87 in K. McRae (ed.) Consociational Democracy. Toronto: McClelland and Stewart.

Steiner, J. (1974) Amicable Agreement. Chapel Hill: University of North Carolina Press.

Tarrow, S. (1976) "From Center to Periphery: Alternative Models of National-Local Policy Impact and an Application to France and Italy," Ithaca: Western Societies Program Occasional Paper, No. 4.

——— (1978) "Introduction," in Tarrow et al (eds.) pp. 1-27 Territorial Politics in Industrial Nations. New York: Praeger.

Toynbee, Arnold (1947) A Study of History, abr. ed. by D.C. Somervell. New York: Dell, Laurel.

Trudeau, P.E. (ed.) (1974) The Asbestos Strike. Toronto: James, Lewis & Samuel.

Van der Esch, B. (1971) Canadian Federalism and the Common Market Formula. Ottawa: Carleton University School of International Affairs.

Van Loon, R.J. and M.S. Whittington (1976) The Canadian Political System: Environment, Structure and Process, 2nd ed. Toronto and Montreal: McGraw-Hill Ryerson.

Verdoodt, Albert (1973) La protection des droits de l'homme dans les Etats plurilingues. Brussels: Editions Labor.

Vile, M.J. (1973) Constitutionalism and the Separation of Powers. Oxford: Clarendon Press.

Watts, R.L. (1970) Multicultural Societies and Federalism. Ottawa: Information Canada.

———— (1966) New Federations: Experiments in the Commonwealth. Oxford: Clarendon Press.

Weitz, Peter (1977) "The CGIL and the PCI: From Subordination to Independent Political Force," pp. 541-74 in D. Blackmer and S. Tarrow (eds.) Communism in Italy and France. Princeton, N.J.: Princeton University Press.

Weller, G.R. (1977) "Hinterland Politics: The Case of Northwestern Ontario," Canadian Journal of Political Science 10:727-54.

Wheare, K.C. (1946) Federal Government. Oxford: Clarendon Press.

White, G., J. Millar and W. Gagne, (1971) "Political Integration in Quebec During the 1960's." Canadian Ethnic Studies 3:55-84.

Wildavsky, Aaron (ed.) (1967) American Federalism in Perspective. Boston: Little, Brown and Company.

Williams, Glen (1979) "The National Policy Tariffs: Industrial Underdevelopment Through Import Substitution," Canadian Journal of Political Science 12:333-368.

Windmuller, J. (1969) Labor Relations in the Netherlands. Ithaca: Cornell University Press.

Wolinetz, S.B. (1973) "Party Re-Alignment in the Netherlands." Ph.D. diss. Yale University.

———— (1978) "The Politics of Non-Accommodation in Canada: Misapplications of Consociational Models and Their Consequences for the Study of National Integration and Political Stability." Paper presented to the Annual Meeting of the Canadian Political Science Association, London, Ontario.

Zolberg, A. (1977) "Splitting the Difference: Federalization without Federalism in Belgium," pp. 103-42 in M. Esman (ed.) Ethnic Conflict in the Western World. Ithaca: Cornell University Press.

———— (1975) "Transformation of Linguistic Ideologies: The Belgian Case," pp. 445-72 in Savard and Vigneault (eds.) Multilingual Political Systems. Quebec: Les Presses de l'Université Laval.